PEACE
THE WORK OF JUSTICE

PEACE
THE WORK OF JUSTICE

ADDRESSES ON THE NORTHERN TRAGEDY
1973 – 1979

CAHAL B. DALY

Veritas Publications Dublin

First published 1979 by
Veritas Publications,
7 & 8 Lower Abbey Street,
Dublin 1.

Cover design by Bill Bolger

ISBN 0 905092 90 2
Cat. No. 3399

Origination by Joe Healy Typesetting, Dublin 2.
Printed in the Republic of Ireland by
Cahill Printers Ltd, Dublin 3.

DEDICATION

Dedicated to the
priests, ministers, lay men and women
of all the Christian Churches
who, through ten tragic years in Northern Ireland,
have risked health, safety, and sometimes life itself
in their determination to be instruments of Christ's peace
and to sow his love wherever there was hatred.

They "never gave in;
never admitted defeat,
they kept on working at the Lord's work always,
knowing that, in the Lord, they could not be labouring in vain."

THANKS

I wish to thank Fr Michael Bannon and Fr Sean Casey who, with my clerical students, Thomas Maguire and Thomas Higgins (helped by John O'Mahony), prepared the index and gave other invaluable assistance. I thank Miss Peggy Gallogly and Miss Siobain Boyle of my office staff, whose dedication and efficiency, going far beyond the line of duty, achieved the "impossible" in typing speed and accuracy in making the material ready for the publishers.

ACKNOWLEDGEMENTS

Grateful acknowledgement is made to authors and publishers for permission to reproduce the following copyright material in this book: an extract from the "The Colony" by John Hewitt in *Community Forum;* extracts from *Religion and Demographic Behaviour in Ireland* by Brendan M. Walsh, published by the Economic and Social Research Institute, Dublin; extracts from "Trends in the Religious Composition of the Population in the Republic of Ireland, 1946-71" by Brendan M. Walsh in *The Economic and Social Review;* an extract from "The Road to Hate" by Patrick Kavanagh from *Collected Poems,* published by Martin Brian and O'Keeffe, London; extracts from "The Second Coming" and "Nineteen Hundred and Nineteen" by W. B. Yeats from *Collected Poems of W. B. Yeats,* published by Macmillan, London; extracts from *One Word of Truth . . .* by Alexander Solzhenitsyn, published by The Bodley Head, London; extracts from *Ancient Christian Writers: the works of St Patrick, St Secundinus* translated by Ludwig Bieler, published by Longman, Green and Co., London; extracts from *Obedience to Authority* by Stanley Milgram, published by Tavistock Press, London; extracts from *The Policies of Legitimacy* by Frank Burton, published by Routledge & Kegan Paul Ltd, London; extracts from "The Sources of Conflict" by James Russell in *The Northern Teacher* and extracts from "Northern Ireland: Socialisation into Conflict" by James Russell in *Social Studies;* an extract from *Facing Death* by Alfred Delp, published by Bloomsbury Publishing Co. Ltd, Stroud, Gloucestershire; an extract from *Raids on the Unspeakable* by Thomas Merton, published by New Directions Publishing Corporation, New York.

CONTENTS

INTRODUCTION

I have collected together in this volume some of the addresses or articles on the tragic problems of Northern Ireland which I delivered or published over the past five years. I had similarly collected and published, in 1973, texts from the preceding five years, in a volume entitled *Violence in Ireland and Christian Conscience.*

The writer has no illusions of special competence in this field. He publishes these papers solely out of a conviction, which has grown stronger with each passing year, that the continuing and even worsening viciousness of violence in the North constitutes one of the gravest dangers facing the Church in Ireland at this time. It threatens our religious and spiritual inheritance, our moral values, our family life, the formation of our youth. It is a danger to the political stability and the economic well-being of the present and of the next generation of the inhabitants of the whole island. The Gospel of Christ has an immediate relevance to this situation. The word of Christ must be spoken to this situation. Who speaks it is of no importance. All that matters is that the word of Christ be spoken at this time of *Kairos* and *Krisis,* this time of judgement and of opportunity, coming from the Lord of history to our country now.

As Father Thomas Merton told us, there are no "innocent bystanders":

> A witness of a crime, who just stands by and makes a mental note of the fact that he is an innocent bystander, tends by that very fact to become an accomplice . . . It is supremely important for us not to yield to despair, abandon ourselves to the "inevitable" and identify ourselves with "them". Our duty is to believe that their way is not "inevitable". ("Letter to an Innocent Bystander" from *Raids on the Unspeakable,* 1964, pp. 53-62).

These texts were written, and are now published, out of a feeling that, if one did not speak out, one might incur the guilt and shame of the silent bystander.

These scripts have been considerably re-worked, revised and updated, and many sections have been transposed. New material has been incorporated. Nevertheless, traces inevitably remain of the original character of the contents, as addresses made on different occasions over a five-year period. For example, a number of central themes are returned to in more than one place. I trust that such repetitions may still serve a purpose, in underlining these themes as central in the discussion and in calling attention to different aspects of these themes.

The texts move, in ways which some might find disconcerting or at least unexpected, from Gospel reflection to political analysis to social and economic consideration; from sermon to prayer to call for political initiative. This is quite deliberate and I make no apology for it. Pope John Paul II has said that the greatest contribution which can be made to man's well-being in society is to lead men back to prayer. The neglect of prayer is the root cause of society's sickness. No one could be a man of prayer and also at the same time a man of violence. Scripture is the mirror into which one must look steadily to see the honest truth about oneself and the unmasked face of one's day-to-day behaviour. Sermons must challenge lived behaviour and life-styles and life-situations, whether personal or social. Sermons must call to repentance, repentance from social sin as well as from personal sin; and repentance means *change,* change of behaviour patterns as well as change of thought-patterns, change of structures and not just change of sentiments. As the Irish Bishops' Pastoral on Justice put it:

> Situations have to be changed as well as souls. Society has to be converted as well as selves. Sanctity has social consequences. So has personal sin.

Prayer, or the neglect of it, has social and, in the broad sense, political implications. Karl Barth has said that every Christian sermon is, in the end, also political. If I may quote Seamus Heaney, in a poem, "Whatever you say, say nothing", from the collection *The North:*

> The times are out of joint
> But I incline as much to rosary beads
>
> As to the jottings and analysis
> Of politicians and newspapermen.

The graffito from a Belfast gable wall, "Is there a life before death?", inspires his concluding verse:

> Is there a life before death? That's chalked up
> In Ballymurphy. Competence with pain,
> Coherent miseries, a bite and sup,
> We hug our little destiny again.

But the last word is not destiny, but hope. There *is* life before death, life that has been through death and defeated it and risen again, new and indestructible, never to die again. There is life that has passed through the valley of the darkness of the tomb and broken through the blackness to be the light of the world, a light the darkness can never extinguish. We must abandon hopelessness, all we who have been allowed to enter into this new life in Christ.

As this book goes to press, Ireland awaits the visit of Pope John Paul, who calls himself "a man of great trust". May Ireland's young people, the hope of our tomorrows, take to heart his words:

> Young people, be builders of peace. . . . Resist the easy ways out which lull you into sad mediocrity; resist the sterile violence in which adults who are not at peace with themselves want to make use of you. Follow the paths suggested by your sense of free giving, of joy at being alive, and of sharing. . . . You are the first victims of war, which breaks your ardour. You are the hope of peace.

+ Cahal B. Daly
1 September 1979

1

NORTHERN TRAGEDY:
CHALLENGE TO THE CHURCHES

There are times when debates cease to be fruitful. Instead of producing light, they only generate emotional heat. Instead of initiating movement, they merely mobilise energies for digging trenches around existing positions. Instead of fostering hope, they tend to make hopelessness respectable by casting the blame for it on others, in the form: "There is nothing to be done, *they* will never change."

This tends to happen when the terms of a question have become so ambiguous that the disputants are really debating different topics. It happens when the terms become so emotive that the disputants are only expressing their resentment of frustration toward the situation or toward each other, rather than hoping to persuade the other or convert him to their point of view. I fear that this is coming to be the case with regard to the questions: "Is the Northern Ireland conflict a religious war? Are the Churches to blame? Why do the Churches not get together and solve the problem?" When debates become sterile, as I suggest this one is becoming, it can be illuminating to try to uncover what motives lead people to ask these questions, what meanings they attach to the terms, what emotions they may be evincing, what attitudes they may be unconsciously defending.

The analysis must, of course, be bilateral and impartial. Unavowed motives and emotions can be operative both in those who affirm that the conflict is religious and that the Churches are to blame, and in those who deny these propositions. As in all such analyses, it is easier to detect the fault of others than to recognise one's own. What we must all realise is that the first requisite for anyone, and above all any Christian, who would speak of the Northern situation, is honesty. Where lives are at stake, there can be no excuse for insincerity.

There should be no excusation for anyone who uses the tragic Northern situation to advance some other cause or interest of his own, whether it be political or theological. Here again, however, one must confess that it is easier to call for utter honesty from others than to detect and eliminate concealed dishonesty in oneself. One can only try.

From frustration to recrimination

The first thing which we should all admit is that, in a situation to which no-one can see a solution, a strong sense of frustration develops. In this mood, people are prone to clutch at any proposal which offers any plausible sign of relevance, and to be impatient and intolerant of those who decline immediately to share their enthusiasm for such alleged remedies. Thus, impatience has been generated, on one side or the other, both by those who say that the Catholic Church could solve the problem by adopting integrated schooling or by revising her mixed marriage regulations, or even by changing her moral teaching on contraception; or who say the Protestant Churches could end the tensions by revising the Thirty-nine Articles or the Westminster Confession; and by those who reject these assertions. The impatience seems to me to be a measure of people's frustration and helplessness in face of the crisis, as much as of their serious conviction that any such proposals are realistic or would solve the problem. A very careful scrutiny of one's own motivations and emotions in these discussions is called for from us all. We must in particular examine ourselves very honestly as to whether we might be invoking the Northern crisis as a convenient prop for a different platform altogether. If people have other causes to promote, they should defend them on their own merits. We in the Republic had fifty years of ritual rhetoric about "the Border", in which the interests were party-political advantage within the Republic, rather than either understanding or concern about the North. The practice still goes on. There is no excuse for it now.

Instead of swopping imputations of guilt and intransigence, it would be better if we all tried to have the humility to recognise that we just do not know with certainty what solutions would succeed; indeed that there is no such thing as "the solution"; but that every relevant suggestion should be examined dispassionately and evaluated objectively. The Church should be setting a headline for others in such exercises. Instead of adopting "all or nothing" postures and rejecting proposals outright because we cannot accept them fully, we should be prepared to distinguish the positive from the negative aspects of any proposal and be ready for some movement towards its aim and spirit, even if we cannot concientiously concede the principle. The only *a priori* condition for dialogue should be a presumption of good faith on the part of "the other side" to the debate. The only *a priori* suspicion should be of those who see all the faults on one side and all the virtue on the other.

Are the Churches to blame?

There are various categories of people who say that the Churches are to blame or are primarily to blame for the situation. Their meanings and motives can be diverse. Politicians may say that the Churches are to blame and that they have it in their power to transform the situation by some theological or legal reforms. It is tempting for the Churches to retort that the politicians are seeking an alibi for their own inertia or failure. This could be partly true. One commentator has remarked, speaking of Dublin politicians: "Their solutions curiously enough are ones which call for sacrifices from other people (e.g. from Catholic Bishops regarding mixed marriages) but hardly any from Dublin politicians." It is probably truer and certainly kinder to say that politicians are baffled and frustrated by the Northern problem, just like other men, and seek to conceal or sublimate their bafflement and frustration by trying to move the focus of interest away from politics to theology or Canon Law. We Irish have anyhow a genius for solving problems by grand speeches, dosed strongly with moral indignation, and for, as the same commentator put it, "offering all help short of aid" which rhetoric can supply.

If the motives of politicians in blaming the Churches can be questioned, however, it is equally incumbent on us churchmen to question the motives which lead us to deny the charge and to refuse blame and responsibility. I think that our first reaction is the feeling that the critics, in this case the politicians, are trying to evade their own responsibility and to find an alibi for their inaction by putting the blame on Church leaders. We tend to retaliate by stressing the political aspect of the problem and emphasising the need for political leadership and political action, for changing structures and institutions. This, I believe, is perfectly valid. Indeed, I would claim that political reforms and social justice are the authentic Christian response, the true contribution of the Churches to the Northern crisis.

Yet I am deeply convinced that the Churches have a certain blame for the genesis of the situation and a real responsibility in regard to it and that they can and do make a real contribution towards resolving it. I firmly believe that both repentance and amendment are required of all of us. But I believe that the true nature and the limits of our blame and our responsibility need to be more precisely defined. I believe also that the true nature of, and above all the severe limitations on, our power as Churches to bring about a solution need to be realistically and humbly admitted. Otherwise, we are in danger of arousing exaggerated expectations, which we lack the power to fulfil; and we expose ourselves to exaggerated accusations, which our degree of blame and guilt do not merit.

I believe further that it would be a distortion of the ecumenical movement in Ireland to relate it too narrowly to the Northern Ireland situation and to evaluate its success or its sincerity in terms of the resolution of the Northern problem. I believe we in the Churches are virtually all united in our abhorrence of political violence from any quarter in Northern Ireland. I believe we are all equally committed to working for peace and justice and reconciliation. But many of us feel that the Northern Ireland problem will itself be misunderstood by one-sided assertion of its religious aspects. Some of us further feel that even its religious aspect can be misrepresented if we insist exclusively on its clerical aspects. Above all, we feel that the pursuit of Christian unity through dialogue is a distinct undertaking from the search for peace in Northern Ireland and that confusing the two could be harmful to both. The criteria for Christian unity and the methods of working towards it are independent of the criteria for what has been called a "united Northern Irish community", not to mention a "United Ireland", and it would be no service to any of these causes to confuse them together.

Ambiguity of the term "the Churches"

Common to much discussion both of the Northern Ireland problem and of inter-Church relations is a reference to the responsibilities and the shortcomings of "the Churches". I believe that behind the use of the term "the Churches" in these contexts can lurk many confusions and much ambiguity. I believe that some semantic clarifications are called for here. First of all, this term could be used and sometimes is used as a camouflaged way of making charges which it is not polite or popular to make openly. I suspect that some people, when they say "the Churches are to blame", really and privately mean that "the Catholic Church" is to blame, or that "the Protestant Churches" are to blame; but they are not prepared to say this publicly. I do not believe that this is helpful. If anyone sincerely believes either of the above statements, he should have the courage and honesty to say so. Sincerity is always less hurtful in the long run than double talk. Criticisms made openly in the presence of the criticised are less offensive and less harmful than criticisms made *in absentia* before an audience of "one's own kind". Even painful criticisms can be healing if spoken honestly and openly in love. No good purpose or impulse, Christian or otherwise, can be served if people say "the Churches have failed", or "Christianity has failed", when what they really mean to claim is that some particular group of churchmen have failed.

This brings me to another ambiguity in the term "the Church" or "the Churches". The term is invariably used in the context in question to refer, not to members of the Churches in general, but to Church leaders. This is for many reasons unfortunate. It reflects a seriously and dangerously defective theology of the Church. It implies that the Church is the clergy or the hierarchy. It suggests that action by the Church is action of an ecclesiastical kind by clergy or bishops, in the domain of the spiritual and the canonical.

It can thus be used as an alibi by laymen to escape their Christian responsibility. It enshrines a false clericalist concept of the Church. It canonises a false "other-worldly" notion of the mission and the action of the Church in the world. It diverts the attention of laymen from the fact that they too are the Church. It ignores the fact that temporal, social and even political action is Christian action. It is vitally important for all of us to realise today that the contribution of Christian politicians, community leaders, editors, journalists, professional people, management, workers, teachers, parents, youth, is a vital part of the total response of the Church to the Irish problem in our time. If "the Church is responsible" were meant in the sense, "all members of the Church are all responsible", then it would be a saving truth for all.

Alas, however, for man's incorrigible capacity for *mauvaise foi*, some who say "we are all responsible", seem really to mean, "all are responsible except me". There is an agreeable glow of moral self-satisfaction to be procured by public confession of the guilt of one's own Church. It is almost always at least half-implied by the penitent and perfectly understood by the audience that it is "the others" who are guilty, but not the penitent. He is "not like the rest". He is absolved by his mere confession, and from penitent becomes judge, finding his fellows guilty from the standpoint of his own moral superiority. It is long since a French writer introduced the phrase, "the pharisaism of the publican". I hasten to add that this is not necessarily or always the case. But it is sometimes the case and always the possibility and danger. Confession is good for the soul; public confession may be good only for the ego. Those of us who indulge in it should earnestly beware of man's limitless faculty for self-deception. Those who say "the Church is to blame", or even "my Church is to blame", should be very careful to ask themselves if what they really want to say is that "my Church's bishops are to blame", or its clergy, or its "bigoted Northeners", or whatever. Even those who say "we are all to blame", may on reflection find that what they really mean is "all are to blame – except me and my fellow-progressives".

A colleague has pointed to some of the confusions lurking in some uses of the term "the Churches" in the context of the Northern situation. He remarks:

Given the different traditions and standpoints of the Churches, it is unlikely that their failures will always coincide. Because we do not wish to say that Church A has failed in this respect, Church B in that respect, etc., we are tempted to say in each case that "the Churches" failed, thereby unjustifiably maximising the extent of the Churches' failures. . . . (The Churches cannot easily be lumped together, since their standpoints are different. For this reason, it seems to me that we should state the record of each Church as fairly as we can, indicating what is positive and negative in its record.)

It seems to me that these points are important and should not be lost sight of when we are discussing the failures and the responsibilities of our different Churches, whether in respect of the Northern tragedy or in respect of inter-Church relations. I think it would not be an unfair analogy to say that to speak of the collective guilt of "the Churches" in respect of Northern Ireland or in respect of inter-Church relations would be just as confusing and as misleading as if we were to lump together all the crimes which have been perpetrated in the history of Anglo-Irish relations and to say that they amount to a massive load of guilt and shame on the part of "the British Isles".

All of us must be on guard not to offend against dispassionateness and objectivity. All proposals, however smugly motivated they appear, however offensively worded they seem to the accused, should be honestly examined with a view to seeing how much of the accusations might be true, or how much of the proposals for reform might be justified. St Paul's admonition that we should "heap coals of fire upon the heads" of our accusers meant the very opposite of returning fiery rebuke for fiery attack. It meant rather being such a person and acting by such standards that the attack is *ipso facto* clearly seen to be unmerited and the accuser is brought to blush for making it and to change his own behaviour in consequence. The situation is too grave for any of us to be content with mere defensiveness or to retreat into hurt self-righteousness.

Positive action by the Churches

It is more profitable to turn from analysing the semantics of the question whether the Churches are to blame to con-

sideration of the positive question of what the Churches can
do to help. Here also a preliminary recall of some of the
moral prerequisites to the discussion seems necessary. A great
humility is called for on the part of all those who from outside the situation would lecture to or about those who
exercise their ministry within it. We must humbly salute the
courage, amounting often to heroism, of the countless clergy
in all the Churches who have laid their reputations, the peace
and safety of their homes, their personal safety and indeed
their lives on the line in riot- and violence-torn areas or in
murder-infested sectors during these past six inglorious years.
Let us not forget that two priests have met their deaths
bringing priestly ministrations to the afflicted under a hail of
bullets. Another was seriously wounded in a failed assassination attempt. Night after violent night, priests and ministers
have gone around anger-filled or panic- and rumour-rife areas
calming emotions, risking the rage of fanatics, speaking
peace amid the flames whether of passions or of fire-bombs.
Ministers have had greater anguish from threats to their loved
ones than from fear for their own persons. It is precisely
where the word of God spoken in and through the Churches
has been most heard that violence has received least support.
It is precisely in areas or among groups who have become
most alienated from the Churches and the least subject to
their influence that the ideologies of violence have found
their most implacable adherents. It should not be forgotten
that it is in the great so-called "Protestant" heartlands of
Belfast and its conurbation, the areas from which U.D.A. or
U.V.F. para-militaries draw their recruits and from which the
sectarian killers emerge, that the percentage of religious
practice is lowest and the influence of the Churches least.

There is also need for historical objectivity in assessing the
influence of religion in the modern history of our country.
Abuse of religion for political ends is not a new development
in this country. It is not of Irish origin either. It is a blot
upon the entire history of British colonial rule in this country,
from its beginnings and right until its concluding chapter.

Sectarianism as we know it in Ireland is in its origin both a
legacy and a consequence of colonialism. I hasten to add that
other imperialisms whether Christian or secular, whether old-
style capitalist or new-style socialist, have practised the same

abuse. I add also that this is not all that colonialism left with us: there were positive features too. Fairness obliges us to add also that sectarianism has survived here long after it virtually disappeared among the original colonisers. It is a characteristic of ex-colonial territories that they retain the mentalities and the prejudices of the colonising country long after the latter has abandoned them.

Several have spoken lately of our "captive Churches". There are indeed respects in which leaders or members of the Churches are, in different ways and degrees, captives of past history or of political ideologies which should now be seen to obscure the true mission of the Church and the authentic meaning of the Gospel. The Church must be undergoing a continual self-examination and purification in order to rid herself of any compromise with the ideologies and "powers of this world".

And yet, when this has been said, it remains true that the Church did not have to wait upon the world to teach us the need for reconciliation and dialogue and the urge to work for a just society. It is arguable that without Pope John the moves towards reconciliation in the North under Lord O'Neill, timid though these can now be seen to have been, and the moves towards reconciliation between the two parts of Ireland pioneered by himself and the late Sean Lemass, could never have taken place. It was in the spirit of Pope John that, in 1958, Catholics met at Garron Tower, under the auspices of the Social Studies Conference, and launched an appeal for Catholics, without compromise of principles, to come forward and take their full part in the life and the service of the community. The Churches Industrial Council, an initiative from the Protestant Churches which was immediately responded to by the late Bishop Mageean, was an early example of inter-Church dialogue, and it made a significant contribution to reconciliation across traditional divides in various industrial and community questions. The Protestant Churches in the mid-1960s began discussing problems, the very existence of which it would have formerly been regarded as disloyal to admit. The Presbyterian General Assembly in 1965 and in 1966 discussed reports about religious discrimination and admitted the reality of grievances among the Catholic community.

Objective reading of history also reminds us that sectarian-ism in its current manifestation first arose by way of protest against the spirit of tolerance and ecumenism which was characteristic of "the Churches". The name of the Rev. Ian K. Paisley first became known through his picketing of the General Assembly of 1966 and refusing subsequently to pay his fine. The Free Presbyterian Church, and the political movement associated with it, were set up precisely by way of protest against the tolerant and ecumenical policies of the contemporary mainstream Protestant Churches and their alleged "softness towards the Church of Rome". Dr Paisley's movement did not originate within the main Protestant Churches but precisely in opposition to them. In order to find freedom of expression, it had to secede from those Churches and finds its greatest boast in that secession. The favourite targets of its abuse, after the Catholic Church, are the main Protestant Churches associated with the World Council of Churches. Its use of the term "Presbyterian" is a constant embarrassment to the Presbyterian Church in Ireland.

The sixties, indeed, are seen in retrospect as a time of promise unprecedented in the earlier history of Northern Ireland. Community attitudes and myths, rigidly frozen for fifty years, were beginning to thaw. The impossible was beginning to seem possible. The reconciling influence of the Churches in all this movement is, I believe, historically undeniable. Dr Paisley was at least an intelligent observer when he saw that the old "No Surrender" Ulster was in danger. He saw too that the danger was coming primarily from the Churches. It was against the Churches that he struck his first blows.

It can, of course, be seen in retrospect that many of the early moves were tentative and qualified. The early reports on discrimination in employment and opportunity, for example, can now be seen as not going very far or conceding very much. Yet we must not minimise their significance by getting them out of perspective. It is fair to gauge their importance by looking at the intensity of the reaction which they promoted. Action and reaction, we once learnt, are equal and opposite. It was not directly political or social causes which first evoked street violence in Belfast and which led to the first appearance of the U.V.F. in the sixties, but precisely the stirrings of the ecumenical movement within the Catholic Church and the main Protestant Churches. It was, I believe, fear of the emergence of a tolerant and just society in the North which led to the first "Protestant backlash". It is arguable that the I.R.A. campaign of the later fifties and early sixties was motivated by the fear that this might conceivably be the last generation in which Catholics would feel sufficiently oppressed and alienated to be sympathetic towards militant republicanism. The campaign failed precisely because the oppression was beginning to be tempered by social welfare and a hope of social justice, and the alienation beginning to yield to a promise of a more tolerant society. In that sense, the republican campaign of 1956 to 1962 came too late for republican hopes. The tragedy of Ulster has been that the lesson of that abortive republican campaign was not grasped by loyalists. It was in great part loyalist intransigence which made possible the next upsurge of republican militancy and ensured its gruesome "successes".

In the late fifties and the early sixties, the sympathies of the minority population in the North lay decidedly not with physical force republicanism, but with what republicans tend now to refer to scornfully as "reformism". The Campaign for Social Justice in Northern Ireland was specifically social and not political in its objectives, and strictly non-violent and in that sense political in its methods. It led in 1968 to the formation of the Civil Rights Movement. For the first time in fifty years, the nationalist minority in the North were united behind a programme of non-violent action whose object was, not to "abolish the Border" or to "destroy Northern Ireland's Constitution", but to secure justice within Northern Ireland.

The tragedy of the early sixties in Northern Ireland was that too little reform was introduced too late to satisfy the minority's reasonable expectations. Too much of the liberal Unionist programme was cosmetic, as though designed to make Unionism respectable rather than to make society really just. That, alas, did not prevent the savage loyalist backlash of August 1969. This backlash was itself only the culmination of a series of violent reactions and repressive measures against the non-violent and in principle non-political

Civil Rights Movement. It was the repression and the backlash which gave the I.R.A. their long-awaited opportunity.

Present political realities
Many of those who were prominent in the Civil Rights
Movement are now leading members of the S.D.L.P.. Extremely
few, if any, I believe, ever belonged to or subsequently joined
the Provisional I.R.A.. This is highly significant. It belies the
loyalist charge that Civil Rights was only a camouflage for
militant republicanism. In the present situation, one of
the great tragedies and dangers is the refusal of the loyalist
political groupings to distinguish between the I.R.A. and the
political parties which attract Catholic membership and
support. The I.R.A. and its political wing might enlighten
them about the difference. The abuse heaped by republican
spokesmen upon the political parties supported by Catholics
is even more virulent than that directed by them against
loyalist politicians.
This, however, does not deter loyalists from identifying
Catholics and even the Catholic Church with the I.R.A.. They
stubbornly persist in lumping all these together as equally
"enemies of Ulster". This strange obsession seems to derive
from or to imply a concept of Catholicism which Catholics
find strange; namely that the Catholic Church is a great
monolithic organisation, controlling the political decisions
as well as the religious beliefs of its members, and ruthlessly
dedicated to the subversion of Ulster and the subjugation of
Protestantism. It seems improbable that men of intelligence,
as the leaders surely are, could sincerely believe these things.
It is not for us to judge to what extent the myths are sincerely
believed or to what extent they are merely found convenient
as the long-proven ways to gathering votes and securing power.
Surely an objective analysis of the political realities of the
past decade would indicate that their most significant feature
has been precisely the emergence of the S.D.L.P. and the
Alliance Party as in their different and sometimes opposed
ways, the electoral expressions of the political aspirations of
a majority of the entire Catholic community in Northern
Ireland; together with the consistent and, indeed, for republicans humiliating rejection by the Catholic electorate of all

species of republicanism. Indeed, one can go further, and say that the related loyalist myth, that religion and politics are inseparable for the Catholic, was given a kind of experimental testing in one recent election. One candidate who went forward explicitly as a Catholic was defeated; even though his record in the struggle for civil rights, both before and since 1969, was outstanding and his tireless advocacy of the rights of the minority and his fearless denunciation of discrimination, internment and British Army harassment, were justly admired. There is just no tradition and no future in Ireland for party-political Catholicism. There is, on the contrary, among Catholics a long-established and jealously-guarded tradition of distinguishing religion from party politics.

The significant truth of the present is, if the loyalists could only see it, that, *for the first time in the whole history of Northern Ireland,* the Catholic community, through their elected representatives, is, in its great majority, firmly committed to working within the Constitution of Northern Ireland, for the pursuit of social justice and equality of opportunity within Northern Ireland. This, when the myth-making and the falsification are given up, is what power-sharing is about. This is even what the much-misrepresented "Irish dimension" is about. These are simply translations for the claim of the minority, as of right, to work within the Constitution, with full recognition of their political identity and rights, but equally with full acceptance of their civic obligations and responsibilities, for a just and tolerant and equal society within Northern Ireland. Their claim to share power is an expression of their desire to share responsibility, to identify with the community and its institutions. Their assertion of the Irish dimension is not disloyalty to Ulster or a threat to Ulster; instead, it is an assertion of their sense of their historic identity as Irish Ulstermen or Ulster Irishmen, just as Britishness is part of the majority's sense of their different historic identity as Ulstermen.

Sectarian or racialist prejudice?

The categorisation of Northern prejudices as religious in origin is sometimes countered by saying that they are due to sectarianism, which is an exploitation of religion for non-religious ends and is, therefore, quite distinct from religion. This I believe, is part of the truth. It is clear to me that the situation is not one of religious war, not one of rival denominational theologies or spiritual allegiances. It is rather one of competing cultures, rival nationalisms, conflicting social classes and economic interest-groups. But "classes" and "interest-groups" are to be understood here not as economic classes in the Marxist-type sense only (for "the working class", etc., is found in both camps), but as historically differentiated groups with economic opportunities and expectations determined broadly by their respective political allegiances, and with their politico-economic differences in turn frequently rationalised into opposing "religious" ideologies.

It is undeniable that denominational affiliations enter into the formation of the respective ideologies. This is why the terms "Catholic" and "Protestant" are a convenient and almost inescapable shorthand for the description of the rival groups. But the use of the terms is sociological, not religious. The explanation of their relevance is to be sought, as suggested earlier, in the past colonial history of Ireland. The situation in Ireland today is a typically post-colonialist situation. The decision by Britain in 1921 to give political institutional expression to religious denominational differences, so far from being a remedy for sectarianism or a formula for peaceful cross-denominational coexistence, proved instead to be the institutionalising of sectarianism. If sectarianism is the conferring of political patronage and preference on the grounds of religious belief, then Britain's solution for the Irish problem, whatever the intentions may have been, was a sectarian solution. It proved to be damaging for both denominational communities. Some perceptive Protestants saw at the time, and others declare today, that it was potentially particularly damaging to Protestantism; for it carried with it a certain danger of Erastian dependence on the State and carried a certain risk of confusion between faith and political ideology. Furthermore, the Partition formula distorted the normal political development of each of the two Irish States and prevented people in both communities from realising the full potential of their common Irish talent for political construction.

To criticise the Partition formula now, however, is not to say that sixty years of history can be reversed by a stroke of some constitutional pen. Separate institutions cannot exist for more than half a century without altering profoundly the very terms of the problems which they were designed to solve. We must go forward from where we are now, rather than seeking to put the clock back.

In the light of the colonialist historical background, however, one could ask if community myths and stereotypes in the North have not also as much in common with racial prejudice as with sectarianism. This might, indeed, be expected from experience of other ex-colonialist countries which have been left with a legacy of community tensions based upon distinctions of colour or race, rather than religion. In Ireland, the situation is compounded by religious distinctions, so that stereotypes which seem typically racialist rather than religious in character become imposed upon people who cannot be distinguished by race or colour and can be identified only by religious affiliation. Study of racial prejudice in different parts of the world can, it seems to me, shed more light upon the Northern problem than can studies of religious prejudice. A colonialist model of our community problems can, I believe, be more relevant than a religious model.

This, I think, is suggested in a striking way in John Hewitt's magnificent poem, "The Colony", written, with extraordinary insight and prescience, in 1950. Here is how Hewitt expresses the stereotypes, the mingled attractions and suspicions through which the descendants of the Planters look towards the descendants of the natives, their fears for their own future, their proud, defiant assertion in face of the natives of their sense of belonging and of their rights:

> They worship Heaven strangely, having rites
> we snigger at, are known as superstitious,
> cunning by nature, never to be trusted,
> given to dancing and a kind of song
> seductive to the ear, a whining sorrow.
> Also they breed like flies. The danger's there;
> when Caesar's old and lays his sceptre down,
> we'll be a little people, well out-numbered.
> Some of us think our leases have run out

but dig square heels in, keep the roads repaired;
and one or two loud voices would restore
the rack, the yellow patch, the curfewed ghetto.
Most try to ignore the question, going their way,
glad to be living, sure that Caesar's word
is Caesar's bond for legions in our need.
Among us, some, beguiled by their sad music,
make common cause with the natives, in their hearts
hoping to win a truce when the tribes assert
their ancient right and take what once was theirs.
Already from other lands the legions ebb
and men no longer know the Roman peace.

Alone I have a harder row to hoe;
I think these natives human, think their code,
though strange to us, and farther from the truth,
only a little so, – to be redeemed
if they themselves rise up against the spells
and fears their celibates surround them with.
I find their symbols good, as such, for me,
when I walk in dark places of the heart;
but name them not to be misunderstood.

. . . .

For we have rights drawn from the soil and sky;
the use, the pace, the patient years of labour,
the rain against the lips, the changing light,
the heavy clay-sucked stride, have altered us;
we would be strangers in the Capitol;
this is our country also, no-where else;
and we shall not be outcast on the world.

Hewitt's gentle, half-admiring, half-wary puzzlement is typical of many. In some, alas, it is replaced by what seems very like racial arrogance, or at best condescension. Religious differences have tended to coincide with social and economic differences. They long overlapped with inequalities in education and career opportunity. Catholics came to be felt as socially inferior. If unemployed or under-privileged, they were thought thriftless and lazy. If receiving social welfare benefits, they were thought ungrateful. If under-represented in higher education or the professions, they were thought under-achievers. The "them-us" mentality reflected socio-economic status or class considerations more than religious differences. I believe the significance of this has not been enough studied. It is said that, during the period of the short-lived Executive, many loyalists suffered real emotional trauma at the thought and the televised sight of having "them" in places of power in "our" Government. Here, it seems to me, is an area where Christian ministers can and should work to evangelise mentalities and emotions with the Gospel message of the obliteration of all inequalities in Christ.

Action by the Churches: the future

I have said that action by the Churches should be directed mainly towards the political and social reforms which are the conditions of a just society and the context of a reconciled society. This action, however, should come, not from the clergy but from the Christian laity. It is no part of the competence of the cleric to compose or to stand on political platforms or to give political directives. The laity too, it must be repeated, are the Church. Their action can never commit the Church as such; they act on their own responsibility, but they act as Christians. It is their vocation as laymen to transmit the message of the Gospel into the temporal and social and political order. Proclaiming the Gospel message is primarily the task of the clergy. Interpreting its social and political implications in terms of concrete political decisions and legislative programmes is the task of the laity. The two roles cannot be confused.

The politics of participation

Social and community problems often have a direct bearing on the violence. The areas from which both sets of para-militaries have come have often been precisely those areas affected or threatened by redevelopment, or resulting from redevelopment displacements. One cannot move around the "ghetto" heartlands or suburbs without realising that our newer housing policies, hardly less than our earlier housing neglects, are sowing seeds of violence. The Catholic Bishops, in their pastoral, *Human Life is Sacred,* have called these policies, with their neglect of the human, the social, the community and the recreational dimensions, "social time-bombs with slow-burning fuses". What I am saying here applies no less to the Republic than it does to Northern Ireland. It is true that housing has to compete with other pressing social needs for scarce budgets. But what we are saving now will be seen to have been a very false and short-lived economy, when society ultimately picks up the bill for the resultant damage. It, quite literally, will be a bill which money cannot pay.

There are other more indirect but no less real connections between the erosion of local community control and democracy and the propensity towards violence. Communities which feel that decisions affecting their lives, their homes, their future, can be taken over their heads and without their knowledge, much less their consultation, by faceless men in distant corridors, on the basis of plans drawn up by remote experts, feel threatened and, because threatened, resentful and aggressive. The modern phenomenon of urban violence seems directly connected with the uprooting of people and the unsettlement of their values by the ceaseless trek from rural areas to cities caused by urban super-growth, the displacement of communities by intra-urban redevelopment, the destruction of local communities, both rural and urban, which both these factors produce, and the resultant de-personalisation whereby people cease to be communities and become instead masses ready for riot. In its causation, as in its manifestations, urban revolutionary violence is not totally different from endemic urban violence. We used, in these respects, to feel superior to far-away cities like Chicago or New York; we are less smug about them now. God grant that we in the South may not need the hard lesson of experience to make us less smugly superior in respect of Northern violence at the present time. We churchmen should be doing all in our power to alert consciences to the causes predispos-ing towards violence in the spheres of political development, social policies and trends, denials of justice and assaults upon the quality of life and the dignity of man in any domain. This continuous struggle for justice and vindication of human rights and dignity, together with commitment to local community development, will, perhaps, be our most effective contribution towards the elimination of violence and the restoration of peace in Northern Ireland and in all of Ireland at this time.

Clerics, the Orange Order and politics

There are, however, areas where clerical practice and party-political action overlap. One of these is the Orange Order; another is the presence of clerics in party politics and in parliament. It is impossible not to sympathise with the feelings of Bishop Richard Hanson when he urged that "Protestants should press for a measure making it illegal for persons styling themselves ministers of religion to sit" (in Parliament). Many Protestants would themselves endorse his further remark that "both Presbyterian and Anglican clergy should eschew membership of and support for the Orange Order and kindred organisations". Indeed many Protestant clergy have risked their futures and their standing among their congregations in refusing membership of the Orange Order. Both of these matters are, however, questions for debate and decision within the concerned Churches themselves. So far as Catholics are concerned, we will do well ourselves to reflect on the Church's teaching as expressed in the Constitution *On the Church in the Modern World* of Vatican II:

> The role and competence of the Church being what it is, she must in no way be confused with the political community, nor bound to any political system. . . . (The Church) does not lodge her hope in privileges conferred by civil authority. . . . But it is always and everywhere legitimate for her to preach the faith with true freedom, to teach her social doctrine, and to discharge her duty among men without hindrance.
>
> She also has the right to pass moral judgments, even on matters touching the political order, whenever basic personal rights or the salvation of souls make such judgments necessary. In so doing, she may use only those helps which accord with the Gospel and with the general welfare as it changes according to time and circumstance. (no. 76).

It is, unfortunately, necessary to remark that a very small number of Catholic priests have from time to time given

grave scandal and offence to Protestants and have seriously
compromised their own priestly ministry by expressing or
displaying support for the I.R.A. or organisations connected
with it. Their conduct is totally reprehensible and has to be
unreservedly condemned. On the other hand, the denunciation of security forces' excesses, of torture etc., can be a
truly priestly witness to the sacrosanctity of human rights
and the dignity of the person, and deserves recognition and
respect as such; all the more so when, as has been the case, it
has been accompanied by equally fearless denunciation of the
crimes of the I.R.A..

It is, rather, at the level of what we may call the evangelical
and moral infrastructure of the political order that the clergy
and hierarchy of the Church should direct their teaching and
sanctifying interest. They should, on the basis of the Gospel
itself, expose and denounce the false judgments, the suspicions, the religious ignorance, which lead to sectarian and
racial prejudice. They should also encourage and support
agencies involved in the analysis of its causes and promote
programmes designed to work for its eradication.

Secularisation and religious ignorance

There are, of course, tasks of a more directly evangelistic
kind which need urgent attention. I believe that not sufficient
attention has been paid, in the Northern Ireland experience,
to the impact of secularisation, in the strict sense of de-
Christianisation, upon the situation. It seems to me that
fanaticism, whether sectarian or revolutionary, is, at least
in modern Western society, characteristic much more of
cultures in which religion has been secularised than of truly
religious cultures. The priests and religious sociologists who
first spoke of "France pagan?" or "France, pays de mission?",
coined the phrase "a pagan country with Christian superstitions". The description seems very apt for both loyalist
and republican para-militaries in the North. In both cases,
if there has not been total alienation, sometimes of many
years standing, from the life and influence of the Churches,
there has been at least a radical secularisation of some areas
of thought, emotion and decision and an habitual, deliberate
and defiant exclusion from them of all influence from the

Church. The former phenomenon is perhaps more characteristic of the loyalist para-military; the latter of the republican.

When religion becomes secularised it tends to become
ideology. Ideologies are religious surrogates. It is characteristic
of them to transfer religious feelings, emotions and fervours
to non-religious causes; to place political programmes in the
category of suprarational truth, which category belongs
properly only to religious dogma. Without the safeguards of
faith and theology, fervour can easily become fanaticism.

There are as many forms of secularised Christianity as
there are of Christianity itself; and there is a distinctively
Catholic as there is a recognisably Protestant way of "secu-
larising". When Irish republicanism "secularises", it invariably
does so in a "Catholic" style; and the style can be confused
with the original Catholicism from which it breaks loose.
There certainly have been in Irish republican tradition some
phenomena which, on deeper analysis, reveal themselves as
unconscious secularisations of Catholic beliefs and attitudes,
Catholic feasts and Catholic rituals. These tend to reinforce
the false surface impression of Irish republicanism as a confessional thing. This at any rate has been how the Protestant
masses in the North have tended to see it and have been
encouraged by their political leaders to see it. Their image
of republicanism has in turn seemed to them to provide
justification and indeed to create the necessity for political
Protestantism.

Loyalist para-militaries can thus convince themselves that
they are fighting for Protestant or even Biblical truths and
values and freedoms. Republicans — while not accepting
religious or denominational labels or motives for what they
do — can persuade themselves that their cause is somehow
sacred or even religious in itself, and that the service of
Ireland absolves and sanctifies anything done in its name.
The republican, in particular, finds sanction from his reading
of history for deliberately separating religion from politics
and deliberately excluding the Church's influence from
revolutionary action. In other words, his conception of
politics and of republicanism, whatever the appearances, is
a radically secularist one. Its fanaticism, like that of the
loyalist, is not religious but secularist in origin.

Re-evangelisation

What the Churches are faced with is, in fact, a massive problem of evangelisation or re-evangelisation: evangelisation of whole groups or areas long estranged from all contact with the Church, long deprived of all influence by the Church's teaching; or re-evangelisation of whole sectors of minds and personalities which have long been radically secularised and closed to the Church's preaching or teaching and influence. The task is intimidatingly difficult. We will have to learn from countries with much earlier experience of the problem than our own. We will have to promote religious education at all levels, child, youth and adult, in school, family and neighbourhood, as well as in church. One of the immediate results of cessation of church-going is religious ignorance. In proportion as people become alienated from the life and worship of the Church, they begin "to make to themselves idols", often taking the form of ideologies, to which they dedicate themselves with similar commitment to that which religious people reserve for God. To use the French expression, these become the superstitions which remain when genuine religious conviction and understanding have been forgotten.

Ecumenical education

A very important and highly relevant dimension of this programme of evangelisation will be the ecumenical dimension. Knowledge of, and initiation in the practice of ecumenism are indispensable elements in all religious education programmes, whether in school or out of school, whether for children or for adults, in any country in the present age, and particularly in our country at this time. I am glad to say that all recent Catholic catechetical syallabi and texts have a resolutely ecumenical orientation. The same is markedly true of the theological formation of candidates for the priesthood. I am sure that the same can be said of all the other Churches. But there remains very much still to be done, particularly at the level of adult religious ecumenical education. A speaker at the third inter-Church meeting at Ballymascanlon called attention to the danger of Church leaders getting distanced from their flocks in the matter of ecumenism. Dialogue between leaders, discussions between theologians, agreements between commissions, must be accompanied by education and involvement of the laity in desire of and prayer for and movement towards mutual understanding, mutual respect and reciprocal reconciliation between divided Christians, which are the prelude, in a time-scale which must rest in the will and providence of God, to ultimate Christian unity.

Even at the level of churchmen, however, mutual understanding, mutual respect and reciprocal reconciliation have not always or everywhere replaced mutual misunderstanding, mutual suspicion and reciprocal imputations of unworthy motives and intentions. Unless we can "kill the hostility", as Christ did, in our own persons, we can give no leadership in killing it in society. Mutual understanding, respect and acceptance between Christians should surely begin among the clergy. Nothing must discourage or deter us from the determination to approach one another with a presumption of the other's good faith, integrity and sincerity, and a respect for his right to be different. We must cultivate, in the words of Father Congar, "an *a priori* of love".

Mutual understanding and respect at religious level will lead to common desire for understanding at the level of communities. It will predispose to efforts, studies, consultations and conversations, designed to reveal how the two divided communities feel about themselves and about one another, to uncover and understand their reciprocal hopes, fears, aspirations and resentments. Loyalists and unionists must try to realise, or better to empathise with, how it feels to be a Catholic, excluded from participation in decision-making and from other normal conditions of fully equal citizenship in his own homeland for fifty years. Nationalists and republicans must try to realise and empathise with loyalists and unionists, who, instead of being secure in power and privilege and social superiority, as Catholics have sometimes thought, are frightened, insecure, disorientated, feeling abandoned by their traditional and trusted leaders, betrayed by Britain, threatened by the Republic, attacked by the I.R.A. – if not, as some imagine, by the entire Catholic community – and perhaps menaced by the dreadful might of Rome! A cartoon published in the North some time ago showed a fearsome figure, festooned with offensive weapons, and captioned, "Protestant fears". The joke had more than one point. Fear stokes violence; insecurity leads to aggressiveness. It is up to all of us, and especially those with responsibility for forming opinion, to do all we can to detect, diagnose and try to allay those fears.

Integrated schooling

"Integrated schooling" is one of the most commonly urged "solutions" for the Northern problem. This is a complex question and is frequently over-simplified. Here I deal with only some aspects, which I believe to be given insufficient attention.

The British Government's Green Paper of November, 1973, *Northern Ireland: Constitutional Proposals,* referred to the question in the following terms:

> One of the obvious factors in the situation is the high degree of educational segregation. This is not of itself in any way peculiar to Northern Ireland. The importance which, in the United Kingdom and in many other countries, certain of the Churches place upon their own school systems stems from deep conviction about the need for an underlying religious basis to all teaching. While, in Northern Ireland, it is the Roman Catholic Church which maintains a separate system, it is by no means to be assumed that, in practice, all Protestant parents would be happy to see a completely integrated school system, involving as it would the teaching of Protestant children by Roman Catholic teachers, some of them members of religious orders. To make the educational system itself the scapegoat for all the ills of Northern Ireland would obscure problems whose origins are of a much more complex character.
>
> There are, however, some encouraging indications of a new consciousness of the need to promote real and continuing points of contact and mutual interest between all the children of Northern Ireland. . . . It will be a vital task of government in the future to facilitate, to encourage and to promote these points of contact. Unless, in the future, a greater sense of community can be fostered amongst the young people of Northern Ireland, it is difficult to see how this mutual distrust can be broken down.

Research into schooling and attitude-formation

The popular debate usually pays scant attention to the findings of research. In fact, an important body of research exists on the question of "integrated education", the work of researchers such as John Darby, John Salters, James Russell; and there is considerable convergence in their conclusions.

Dr James Russell, for example, has been led to stress "the importance of community rather than school influence". He asserts:

> In Northern Ireland there has been a renewed questioning of the liberal assumption that separate schooling is largely to blame for community tensions and disorders. For example, segregated housing estates, the formation of large gangs, para-military groups and discordant adult-created youth groups, have been seen as being much more effective in socialising conflicting cultural types, within Northern Ireland, than have the schools.

Analysis of the research results convinced Russell that inter-community attitudes and relationships among children are determined much more by their families and neighbourhoods than by their schools. Basic political assumptions and social identities seem already to have been assimilated by the children by ages eight or ten. Proneness to violence seems to be a function of children's attachment to gangs and adult-sponsored organisations, rather than of their schooling. Russell finds that "the community, rather than the school, is the chief socialiser of divisive political content".

> Outside of the school, family, social class, national community, religion, local political influences, peer-groups, adult-created youth movements, para-military organisations, and violent events, continue to shape the civic character of Ulster schoolboys.

Russell finishes with some strongly-worded conclusions:

> Given the high likelihood that parents and religious leaders will object to their children being taught by Orangemen or Republicans indiscriminately, integration may simply involve the two-way movement of pupils and teachers without pupils being taught by someone of the opposite religion. Such a situation could involve playground battle-scenes that could make street riots appear as minor incidents.
>
> The consequences of forcibly using integrated schooling in an attempt to unite different communities, without community co-operation, will probably end by driving them further apart. The problems connected with creating mixed housing areas and/or bussing pupils and teachers with different religious complexions

may provide confrontations and levels of intimidation as yet unseen
in Northern Ireland. Thus, it ill behoves those who have not moved
to touch English or Scottish religious schools, or to nationalise
public schools, to lecture Ulstermen about integrated education.
In the event of integrated schooling, this will come after a solution
at the community level. Prior to ending the conflict, any attempt to
integrate may only increase conflict. Seeing integration as a palliative
which would ease, if not attack, the roots of community divisions,
fails to take account of the community obstacles to common
schooling.

These judgements of Russell are the more impressive in
that, as he recounts, he came to Northern Ireland in the
1960s sharing "the popular assumption that separate schooling for Protestants and Catholics leads to, or at least reinforces, discord, disorder and consequent violence". His
research convinced him that this popular assumption is at
variance with the facts. It even distracts attention from the
real causes of discord and the real directions along which
solutions must be sought. If children's community attitudes
are assimilated from the political and social attitudes of their
families and their adult environment in neighbourhood and in
society generally, then solutions can be found only at the
same political and social events.

Thus, it is unrealistic to expect schools to create attitudes in pupils
which are conducive to common allegiance in Northern Ireland, in
the absence of support from the adult community and the existence
of a political institution which is generally accepted as fair and
impartial. . .
   Only when there is some fundamental agreement on a political
structure for Northern Ireland, can we expect the main general
agents of socialisation to provide experiences that will gradually
combine to determine how an individual will play his role as a
citizen.

To those who point to instances in which integrated schooling is working with apparently satisfactory inter-community
results, Russell replies:

Where integrated schooling appears possible because there are few
visible signs of discord, it may simply be irrelevant as far as reducing
conflict is concerned. Or, in other words, where integrated education
is possible it is unnecessary, because religious communities can
tolerate each others' differences.

Social, economic and political dimensions

Russell has called attention to the divergent expectations in respect of "integrated schooling", which are entertained by different social or religious groups favouring integration. He remarks:

> Protestants may see it as a way of getting rid of Catholic schools and inculcating loyalty to Northern Ireland, thus ensuring the predominance of their way of life. Catholics, on the other hand, may see integrated education as a good means towards economic advantage, conversions of Protestants through marriage, and eventual absorption of the Protestant community into a United Ireland.

Clearly, the social and political assumptions and objectives of those who favour school integration need to be scrutinised. If, and insofar as, some sectors of opinion see in integrated schooling a way of creating a "united Ulster community", "a common Ulster allegiance", etc., one would have to ask to what extent this represents, or at least is certain to be seen by the other community as representing, a bid by the larger of the two historic communities in Northern Ireland to assimilate or absorb the other; for such conceptions of "Ulster" completely beg the central historical, political and cultural question, "Which Ulster?". What looks at first to be a disinterested programme for reducing community tensions could easily be seen as a further threat of dominance of one tradition over the other, and could therefore merely increase community tensions. It could easily come to be interpreted as "educational engineering" or indoctrination for political ends. This fear would be likely to be aggravated by suspicion that the Catholic community was being faced with the danger of being unjustly deprived of control of schools for the provision of which, out of religious conviction, they had made enormous financial sacrifices. This could easily be seen as one more instance of injustice and discrimination.

The invoking of integrated schooling as a remedy for Northern Ireland's ills could furthermore divert attention from the socio-economic realities associated with community divisions. It cannot be regarded as irrelevant that, if a series of maps were prepared, indicating respectively the distribution of unemployment, and the areas of origination and perpetration of acts or scenes of destruction and violence, the areas of white, grey and black would show a disturbing overlap.

Some of the school-based research to which I have been calling attention uncovers deep layers of resentment in the minority community with regard to the undue burdens of poverty and deprivation, unemployment and lack of social and economic opportunity, which have been the experience of large sections of this community for many generations. Until these resentments are removed or at least reduced, by vigorous social and economic measures to correct their causes, there is no hope that school programmes will redirect attitudes. Attitudes are in greatest part determined by social situations and environmental realities, rather than by school programmes.

Above all, resentments in the minority community derive from its permanent, unchanging and apparently unchangeable experience of being excluded from the decision-making processes of government. This inevitably fosters a sense of alienation, of not belonging, of being "against the Government", "against the Establishment", which has always been, and seems always intended to continue to be, "them", and never "us". One does not have to be a social psychologist to realise that this experience creates very serious obstacles to the development of a sense of identification with the institutions and organs and agencies of government. This is basically a political problem, for which political solutions must be sought. As James Russell puts it:

> In other words, political institutions must be sought which would, "accept the differences in aspiration and religion on a separate-but-equal basis and try to regulate the conflict".

But this is not to say that nothing can or need be done educationally to reduce inter-community tensions, alleviate mutual fears or allay reciprocal suspicions. There exists in fact an agreed inter-Church statement of policy on the matter of schooling, which offers a way of escaping from sterile polemic into positive collaborative action. I refer to the Report, *Violence in Ireland,* submitted by a joint working party to all the main Churches in 1976. The agreed suggestions on pages 86-87 would go very far to achieve the benefits claimed, without supporting evidence, for "integrated education" without loss of the proven benefits of Church-related education. Surely this is the way forward. The discussion is about helping young people to transcend ghettoised mentalities and relate to each other in mutual understanding and respect across ancestral barriers. That is the end to which all participants to the integration discussion are committed. Let us concentrate on finding relevant means for bringing the end about within each system and between the two systems. It is a matter for school management authorities, with the help of educationists, to research the types of programme and activities, and to determine the levels and the forms of sharing and exchange, which offer best hope of contributing effectively to the desired end. It is no time for sulking in tents. It is better to light one candle than to curse others for the darkness.

Mixed marriages

Sometimes linked with the pressure for "integrated schooling", but strongly urged also in its own right, is demand for relaxation of the Catholic Church's regulations on inter-Church marriages or "mixed marriages". The Catholic Church has in fact introduced important changes in her legislation in this matter. The celebrated "Ne Temere" Decree has been revoked. Since 1970, the Church's requirements are those formulated in the Motu Proprio, *Matrimonia Mixta.* This certainly did not fully satisfy Protestant wishes in respect of inter-Church marriages; but it is important to recognise just how genuine was the Catholic Church's desire to detect and to remove what caused offence to Protestants. The Church of Ireland bishops issued a Pastoral Letter in November 1966, with reference to the then current legislation, contained in the Roman *Instruction on Mixed Marriages* of the same year. "The *Instruction*", the Bishops declared, "is unacceptable because it requires as a condition of the marriage a promise from the Church of Ireland partner whereby all the children born of the marriage are claimed for the Roman Catholic Church."

In virtue of the 1970 legislation, no promise, whether written or verbal, is now asked for from the Protestant partner. The Catholic is asked to recognise and acknowledge that he, as a Catholic, has a grave obligation from God to do all in his power to have all his children baptised and brought up as Catholics. This is the only reason why a promise is required now, and it is required of the Catholic only. The Church is surely not exceeding her right here. She is merely fulfilling her duty of reminding her subjects of what she firmly believes to be God's law. For the Catholic Church believes, as the Motu Proprio states, that this obligation of the Catholic "is imposed by divine law, namely by the plan of salvation instituted through Christ"; and she further believes that she, the Church, can never remove this obligation. The Catholic Church's attitude can never be understood if it is interpreted in political or demographic or sociological terms. It is a question of doctrine, of ecclesiology, of how the Church understands herself.

The leading authority in this field is Brendan M. Walsh, who has written two papers on the matter. His first paper, *Religion and Demographic Behaviour in Ireland,* (Economic and Social Research Institute, Dublin, May 1970), does single out mixed marriages as a major factor in the decline of the Protestant population of the Republic. He says:

> While these calculations are quite tentative and approximate, they do serve to establish conclusively that, in 1961 at least, mixed marriages had a major impact on the demographic position of the 'Other Denominations' population of the Republic of Ireland (p. 27).

He also points, however, to such other dimensions of the phenomenon as the unusually low marriage rate and the exceptionally low birth rate prevailing in the Protestant part of the Republic's population. The birth rate, he says, "is extremely low by any standards". He goes on to point out that internationally the only recorded rate which was lower was that of Hungary in the early 1960s; but Hungary's rate subsequently rose. Walsh comments: "The low 'Other Denominations' birth rate obviously raises the question whether the population is being replaced" (*Op. cit.,* p. 14). Furthermore, the Protestant population is characterised by a very much older than usual average age and has a consequently high death rate.

Walsh's study deals mainly with the statistical picture presented by the years 1946 to 1961. He does not, therefore, touch on factors from an earlier period which clearly had a major impact on Protestant population trends. Such were, in particular, the very high casualty rate among Protestants fighting with the British Army in the First World War, a casualty rate which had relatively far greater impact on the Protestant than on the Catholic population, because of the minority status of Protestants in the counties now comprising the Republic. Another significant factor was the high rate of emigration among the Protestant population in the early decades of Irish independence, an outflow which relatively affected this community more than the Catholic population, since the latter, although it, too, suffered heavy emigration, was much larger to start with. It took quite a number of decades before the Protestant population finally adjusted itself to the changed conditions in Ireland and fully accepted the part in the building of the independent Irish State which, happily, the leaders of that State had, from the outset, been manifestly anxious to accord to them. Indeed, there seem at the present time to be reassuring indications that the Protestant population of the Republic is once again stabilising itself and even, perhaps, tending to recover – a happy consequence, one hopes, of the new confidence among Protestants in the institutions of the Republic and of their unquestioning acceptance of their Irish identity.

A further feature of mixed marriages which is not often recalled in the discussion is the extent to which mixed marriages operate as a factor of "leakage" and loss to the Roman Catholic population. Every pastor is aware of this aspect of the problem; but it has not been quantified. More research is therefore needed.

Brendan Walsh has devoted a second study to the problem, entitled "Trends in the Religious Composition of the Population in the Republic of Ireland, 1946-71" (*The Economic and Social Review,* July, 1975). In this second study he still finds that:

> the evidence . . . establishes, fairly conclusively in my opinion, that mixed marriages have been an important phenomenon for the non-Roman Catholic population of the Republic between 1961 and 1971, and probably also at earlier dates. It seems that the Church of Ireland in particular has been seriously affected by this phenomenon (*Op. cit.,* p. 553).

Speaking of the effect of mixed marriages on the birth rate, however, he now states:

> In my earlier study I presented similar, although less detailed, evidence on mixed marriages for 1961. On the basis of this evidence, I inferred that this phenomenon had an impact on the Protestant birth rate because the off-spring of mixed marriages would tend to be raised as Roman Catholics. I am less convinced now that there is any *statistical* evidence to warrant this inference.
>
> . . . We cannot conclude on the basis of the available evidence, that the phenomenon of mixed marriages has had a serious impact on the Church of Ireland birth rate (*Op. cit.,* p. 554).

His conclusion is:

> The decline in the numbers of Protestants since 1961 has been due to two main factors:
>
> (a) A high death rate – the result of an abnormally aged population as a consequence of long-term population decline.
>
> (b) A low birth rate – also due in part to the abnormal age structure, but partly to a relatively small average family size (*Op. cit.,* p. 555).

Meanwhile, scientific objectivity surely indicates a need for prudence concerning the various hypotheses and requires care and moderation in public utterances regarding the impact of mixed marriages on Protestant population decline.

There is neither justification nor excuse for the use of emotive slogans, such as "religious genocide", which have sometimes been put in circulation. Concern for the future of the Protestant population of the Republic would urge that factors other than mixed marriages would also be given due attention. Undue concentration on the mixed marriages factor alone could prevent the search for remedies for the other factors.

It is intriguing to note that researchers agree that mixed marriages have no demographic importance in Northern Ireland. The population problems of Protestants in the Republic seem linked to and inseparable from their being a numerically very small group and a proportionately very small percentage of the total population, artificially cut off from the preponderantly major portions of their respective Church communities in Northern Ireland. These problems are also found to be independent of the comparatively favoured economic position of Protestants in the Republic. If this is so, then the complex factors producing a decline in the Protestant population may prove to be the inevitable consequences of the partition of Ireland.

Irish bishops' application of the Motu Proprio

The view is expressed that the Irish Eposcopal Conference has taken a "hard-line" position in its interpretation and application of the Motu Proprio. In support of this it is urged that the Irish Bishops have stressed the Catholic's obligation by divine law to do all in his power to secure the Catholic upbringing of all the children; and that this insistence leads to a restrictive pastoral practice. It must be emphasised, however, that this is not an interpretation of the Motu Proprio but merely its plain text, as the quotation above shows. Moreover, in this, the Motu Proprio was simply implementing the decisions of the Synod of Bishops of October 1967 and the wishes of the world-wide episcopate. Father Congar, replying to criticisms of the Motu Proprio by Father Hans Küng, said that "few documents have obeyed the demands of collegiality more than the Motu Proprio in question".

Comparison of the post-Motu-Proprio statements and pastoral practice in Ireland with those obtaining in England and Wales, Scotland, Australia, New Zealand, indeed the English-speaking world as a whole, reveals no significant difference.

We bishops would most earnestly wish it to be accepted that it is reasons of conscience, and reasons of conscience alone, which have guided us in our thinking and our practice in respect of inter-Church marriages. We are anxious to do everything that conscience allows, in dialogue and co-operation with other Churches, to make the problems of mixed marriages less hurtful to relations between the Churches and less painful for the partners of inter-Church marriages.

From mutual destruction to dialogue

In Northern Ireland at this time, for the two communities to talk with one another is not alone the only alternative to destroying one another; it is also the only way to arrest a steady slide into barbarism. As surely as talking separates men from the beasts, so does solving problems by talking, rather than by killing or terrorising, distinguish the civilised from the brutal society. It is not accidental that the word "parley" is used for settling violent disputes, or that the word "parliament" is the mark of a mature, democratic society. Those who derisively call parliament "a talking shop", are unconsciously paying it a tribute. Even at its worst, a "talking shop" is better than a "bomb-and-bullet-shop".

"Talking with", however, is different from "talking at". Dialogue is one thing, lecturing is another, hectoring or haranguing yet another. We have had too much in Ireland of all varieties of noise other than "talking with".

It is not easy for Irishmen to resist the temptation to "talk at", or "talk down", or even "talk-drown". We have another fatal habit in Ireland, that of "talking over our own shoulders" to applauding followers, in the hope of hearing them, when we are safely back "among our own", saying: "He didn't let our side down; he gave it to them good and strong." We Irish are great talkers. But we are bad listeners. We speak for our own side. We seldom listen to the other; or do so only impatiently, waiting our chance to interrupt and get in with the refutation and the self-justification. "Talking with" is as much, perhaps even more, listening than speaking. It questions the other: but even more it questions ourselves, our own side, our own kind. The value and authenticity of Catholic-Protestant dialogue can be measured by the degree of listening that is evident in the intervals between the sentences or the spaces between the lines.

Both parts of Ireland are now part of the European Community. This carries its message of hope. One lesson we can get from Europe is that reconciliation between historic enemies is possible. It is possible between nations. It is still more possible between Churches. Protestants and Catholics in Germany and in Holland were still more deeply opposed, still more embittered, than Protestants and Catholics in the North of Ireland. The speed and degree of reconciliation which has been accomplished in these two countries would, twenty years ago, have been unbelievable. The Holy Spirit is a mighty, creative, re-creative and healing power. He can work in strange ways. Incredibly, and contrary to all his intentions, Hitler was an agent of ecumenical reconciliation. Unity of Christian hearts was forged in the cauldron of Nazi violence. The violence which Irish Protestants and Irish Catholics have suffered in the past six years can be a crucible of reconciliation for us too. Our suffering can be redemptive. It can be reconciliatory. But it will be so only to the extent that we "suffer with" each other as if the other's suffering were our own. "Suffer with" is the strong, original meaning of "sympathise". Catholics must, in this strong sense, sympathise with Protestant sufferings, fears, insecurities; Protestants must sympathise with Catholic insecurities, fears, sufferings. That is how we "complete in our flesh what is lacking in Christ's afflictions" for the sake of all our Churches.

THE POLITICS OF PEACE

In our country, given its history of colonial-type government, revolutionary violence and colonialist counter-violence, the question of attitudes towards political violence becomes a key moral issue for every politician and indeed for every Christian. Historically, both parts of Ireland and both religio-cultural communities in Ireland have been involved in or associated with political violence. On the one hand there has been the struggle of nationalist Ireland first for survival and then for political and civil rights and finally for freedom from imperialist domination. This struggle, although many of its best and most productive phases were non-violent, often took on a violent revolutionary form. On the other hand there was the struggle of loyalist Ireland to preserve the imperial connection and United Kingdom status, first for all Ireland, then, when this proved impossible, for as much of Ireland as could be held for a loyalist majority.

It would be churlish and chauvinist to deny that the loyalist tradition made positive contributions to Ireland's welfare, from which both populations have benefitted; that it left us, even in the Republic, with cultural and other institutions from which we still profit; and that it later brought economic and social benefits to Northern Ireland in which both communities shared. But this loyalist tradition rested on violence, designed first to repress the nationalist and separatist movement in all of Ireland, and later, when this failed over most of the country, to assert and preserve loyalist ascendancy over the North-Eastern counties. History gives no sort of justification to the view that violence or "terrorism" have character-ised or now characterise one Irish community or tradition more than another. Both Irish States owe their origin to revolutionary struggle; and it is prejudice which calls one revolution terrorism and the other loyalism.

It is widely recognised that our subsequent attitudes to political violence in both parts of Ireland have been ambivalent. Orators in both areas, whether political, politico-clerical or other, had their familiar cues for the set speeches on the past glories of violence or even the possible future need for violence. Frequently enough, nothing but the rhetoric was ever meant to be violent. The eventual pay-off was intended and expected to be personal or party political advantage, not bloodshed; votes, not bullets. Once more, it is not possible to put one Irish tradition in moral quarantine and exonerate the other. The dishonours are equally shared.

The experience of the past eight years, however, compel us to now ask how far the past conventional rhetoric of some Southern political platforms and of Northern "Twelfth demonstrations" and other occasions contributed to creating a mood by which the sorrows and crimes in Ulster today were made possible. Yeats asked himself whether certain verses of his could possibly have sent men out to die. Orators and politicians, and particularly, because of their special position, politician-clerics, must ask themselves now whether speeches or writings of theirs are sending men and youths to murder and die, or inciting communities to the suspicion and fear which lead to intimidation and mutual destruction. David did not kill Uriah. He only created conditions in which Uriah's death became "inevitable and unavoidable". This did not deter the prophet Nathan from calling him the murderer, in the unforgettable words: "You are that man." It is time that laws against incitement to racial or religious prejudice, hatred or violence were made effective and were enforced. People were undoubtedly interned for less than the guilt of many active and recent inciters to hate and violence.

Ulster's future

The horrible wave of sectarian destruction and murder which swept Northern Ireland at various times in these recent years will have, at dreadful cost in sorrow and fear, at least produced some good effect if it leads to a re-appraisal of attitudes to violence in the majority community as well as in the minority community in Northern Ireland. It removes the last justification for the one-sided use of the term "terrorist" as a description of republican militants. It exposes as without excuse any security policy which would regard certain minority areas as "terrorist" areas while leaving others to be regarded as safe for "law and order". Terrorism has been revealed as a pathology crossing political and religious boundaries. It can no longer be seen as the evil of one community which the other community must crush. It is the common evil threatening both communities alike with destruction. Loyalism and terrorism are not opposites. Loyalist terrorism is an indisputable fact. Terrorism is the work of a fractional minority in the loyalist camp as it is in the nationalist camp. Perhaps both sides will have learnt now that it is un-Christian to blame a whole community for the misdeeds of a few.

It can be a beginning of truth and of repentance when we all realise that the guilt of violence and the propensity to violence are to be found on both sides. Equally the condemnation of violence and the struggle against violence are found on both sides. A new mood of humility and sense of shared guilt might help to lead us to a new beginning. Perhaps the most important lesson is that we must begin to think not of "sides" but of people. We need a new criterion of patriotism, a new test of loyalty — namely respect for and love of people. The test can be our use of the terms "the people of Northern Ireland", "our people in the North". Unless people in each tradition deliberately and clearly include the people of the other tradition every time they use these phrases, then they are revealing unconscious sectarian bias in their thinking. Unless leaders in each community consciously and earnestly try to talk to and with people of the other community as well as their own supporters, then they are not leaders but frightened followers of their community's prejudices. We have talked at and about "the other sort" long enough. When we talk publicly to them, we are still too often talking through them to "our own people" behind their backs.

There is a frightening tendency in both militant camps to discredit talks and politicians who take part in inter-party talks. Talk is the very basis of politics and of society. Parliament is originally the place where people talk. To deride talk is to discredit political institutions and ultimately to despise both people and democracy. To find a parallel to this kind of language one would have to turn to Germany of the early thirties. Whatever their ideological protestations, such persons share a common contempt for democracy and for people.

It is the witness both of the dead and of the living that such policies lead only to disaster for both communities. Two thousand dead in ten years are surely enough to show how cheap persons have been held in comparison with slogans. Behind each corpse what a *cortège* stretches out of sorrow and deprivation, broken hearts, broken families and broken lives. How many thousands more are either "opting out" in utter weariness of the struggle for inter-community peace; or are emigrating as a final declaration that our country offers them no endurable present and no acceptable future. Ireland has long know the evil of emigration from economic necessity. Now Northern Ireland is experiencing a new kind of emigration, the emigration of social and moral despair. All too often, it is the best who go. What they will give to other lands is precisely what their own land needs from them but does not seem ready to accept. Like so many Irishmen and Ulstermen before them, our new emigrants will discover one another in exile as fellow-Irishmen who will wonder what all the fear and hatred in the homeland were about.

The death, the destruction, the exile will continue until politics is re-established as honourable and patriotic and until credible political institutions take the place of violence. One of the names for justice and consequently for peace in Northern Ireland today is power-sharing. Fifty years of unreconciled communities and recurrent community violence have shown that power unshared cannot survive and has no future. Those who obstruct power-sharing and try to sabotage movement towards new political institutions today are sabotaging the future of both Northern Ireland communities. They are guilty of a crime against both their own tradition and that of the other community; indeed of a crime against the Irish and against the Ulster peoples.

Republican violence

Insofar as republican violence is concerned, since this is often claimed to be in defence and protection of the Catholic areas, it is time that it was recognised that the net result of ten years of violence to date is that these same Catholic areas are now weaker and more demoralised, more oppressed and depressed, more uncertain of their future and more fearful for their survival than they have ever been. Some of the oldest and most beloved Catholic areas in Belfast have been reduced by intimidation and fear to their smallest numbers and lowest morale for many decades. I do not hesitate to say that Catholics are the first victims and the chief casualties of the very violence which is alleged to be waged in their defence. Economically weaker as they always have been, it is the Catholics who will have the weakest capacity for recovery when the violence sometime ends.

Let no one say that I am making a "sectarian" plea. I am not ignoring the sufferings caused to Protestants nor am I less concerned for them. I refer to the suffering of Catholics because I am speaking of that part of the spiral of violence which originates from republicans and which is supposed to be in protection of Catholics.

An enormous responsibility before God and before history rests on the consciences of that small group of men who have had it in their power to order the cessation of violence. Nobody should any longer doubt their movement's power to continue the campaign for just as long as they choose to continue it. There is no way in which they can be defeated. The methods too often used by the British Army and security forces to defeat them are in fact in many cases their greatest source of propaganda material and their greatest recruitment appeal.

The republican leadership cannot be defeated. Where they are mistaken is in thinking that not to be defeated is the same thing as to win. It can sometimes be so. But in this case, it is far from being so. For every year in which they are militarily undefeated, the welfare of the very people they claim to be liberating is set back by perhaps ten years.

I do not need to repeat my unswerving conviction that the present republican campaign of violence is immoral and evil. I want deliberately to confine myself here to its history and strategy. The temptation of a revolutionary movement is to think that because their violence has seemed to produce some of the results they intended, more violence will inevitably produce more positive results and eventually achieve a complete solution. This by no means follows. History shows that very few revolutions have been halted in time, their second phase has in fact usually been totally destructive of whatever positive results the first phase has achieved. The second phase of most of the revolutions of history has been in the most exact sense counter-revolutionary. The republican revolutionaries of our time seem fatally, if not fatalistically, bent on pursuing the same self-destructive course.

At the most, all that further violence can do is to go blindly and fanatically on; and there seems no certain reason why it could not go on for ten more weary years. If it does, it may produce a solution, but the solution may be the opposite of that intended. The solution could be the achievement of the extremist loyalist dream of a "final solution", namely the corraling of the Catholic minority in Belfast into a single ghetto in West Belfast, where they can be isolated, economically deprived and socially exiled; and the confining of the Catholics of the rest of the Six Counties into areas West of the Bann, while industrial development would be concentrated in the loyalist preserve of the North-East corner. This is one horrible and perfectly possible result of the republican campaign of violence. Thus, incongruously, the republican aim to "liberate" the repressed minority of the North would have served only to bring to pass the traditional loyalist aim of subjugating that minority finally and permanently.

May the republican leadership be moved to draw back from that brink before it is too late. The only possible hope of honourable survival for a minority outnumbered two to one lies in skilled and courageous use of political intelligence. The Northern minority have proven that they have the intelligence, skill and integrity needed to win for themselves as of right and on merit an equal place in society. The republican militarists have chosen the one way in which the Northern minority are bound in the circumstances to fail, the way of violence. They have rejected the one way in which that minority could succeed in securing justice and equality of civil rights, the way of political action.

Ulster's many dimensions

The politics which must rebuild on the ruins left by violence is not the politics of flag-wavers and drum-bashers, whether orange or green, for this belongs to a past which led us to our present shambles. The politics we require now is one dedicated to the real needs of living people now. For far too long in Northern Ireland we have been congealed in an ideological deep-freeze: on the one hand, all doors "banged, barred and bolted" since 1912; on the other, all structures treated as null and all developments declared non-existent except the "indestructible Republic" of 1916. Each attitude is equally and very literally backward-looking. The two have inevitably turned into twin pillars of very bitter and totally sterile salt.

There can be no hope of peace without new political institutions; and no new political institutions can bring peace unless they are such as to give institutional expression to all the interlocking dimensions of the total Ulster political and cultural situation. Institutional expression must be given to power-sharing, which in the special Northern Ireland situation is the only viable form of democracy; to British dimension, Irish dimension and Ulster dimension; to equality of civil rights, of social opportunity and of cultural expression; all these dimensions entailing, it must be added, correlative co-responsibility for the common good. A further dimension, so important that it needs separate mention, is that of impartial policing, divorced from military and political security systems and freed of the unhappy associations and memories which policing in the past had for a section of the population.

"Ulster dimension"

I mentioned the "Ulster dimension"; but it is important to remember that there are two kinds of Ulster loyalty, the "British Ulster" loyalty and the "Irish Ulster" loyalty. The former is not true to itself if it does not include attachment to the British link. The latter is not true to itself if it does not include the Irish unity aspiration. The two Ulster loyalties are distinct, but they need not be and must not be exclusive of nor antithetic to one another. Analysts of the Northern situation have very seldom adverted to the highly important and relevant fact that there are two quite distinct kinds of Ulster regional loyalty, one which we have called "British Ulster" and the other "Irish Ulster". We have been hearing lately a good deal of talk about a common "Ulster identity", which is supposed to characterise both communities in Northern Ireland and to mark them as together distinct from the Irish identity of the rest of the island. Apart from the obvious fact that three counties within the territory of the Republic share in whatever is meant by the "common Ulster identity", this language ignores the obvious fact that there are two distinct forms of "Ulster identity", forms which are distinct historically, culturally, politically and socially. Each group understands and lives its Ulster identity, in all the ways which are politically relevant, quite differently from the other. There is, to repeat, an "Irish Ulster identity", and there is a "British Ulster identity".

The British Government has itself equivalently recognised the existence of these two identities and their relevance to the problems of Northern Ireland. The Green Paper, *The Future of Northern Ireland,* discerns the inherent defect of Northern Ireland's political institutions for fifty years, seeing this as residing in the fact that these institutions and the resultant conventions did not take account of the "special feature of the Northern Ireland situation, (namely) that the great divide in political life was not between different viewpoints . . . but between two whole communities". These institutions, in fact, led to the creation of a "permanent majority", unlikely to develop sensitivity, and a "permanent minority" unlikely to develop responsibility.

This same document marks an historic breakthrough in Westminster-Northern Ireland relationships also in that it officially recognises the "Irish dimension" of the Northern Ireland problem. It does indeed reiterate the long-standing Westminster pledge regarding the "constitutional position" of Northern Ireland; but it expressly states that this does not "preclude the necessary taking into account of . . . the Irish dimension". There is even recognition of "the possibility − which would have to be compatible with the principle of consent − of subsequent change in the status"

This Green Paper represents the most penetrating analysis

ever to have emanated from a British Government source of
the Irish and the Ulster problem. It is tragic that this level of
understanding should not have been matched subsequently
by an equal level of political sagacity and competence. The
Green Paper could and should have inaugurated a completely
new chapter in the long and sad history of British-Irish
relationships; instead it was succeeded by political indecision,
stagnation, and blunder alternating with bluster, which have
disappointed and demoralised both communities.

The much-contested "Irish dimension", therefore, is not
some "outside interference" in Ulster affairs; it is an internal
Ulster reality, inherent in the "Irish Ulster" tradition. Similarly, Ulster nationalists must acknowledge the British
dimension of politics in Northern Ireland. This British
dimension must be unreservedly acknowledged as an integral
part of the Ulster reality. It is absurd to speak of this British
dimension as some form of "foreign occupation" of Irish
territory. As has been frequently pointed out, people of the
"British Ulster" tradition have been longer in Ireland than
any white men have been in the United States of America.
Both "sides" must remember that the internal Irish dimension in Ulster has no more right to exist than the internal
British dimension, but also no less. Both sides must remember that the internal British dimension in Ulster has no less
right to exist than the internal Irish dimension, but also no
more. Furthermore, when nationalists acknowledge this
British dimension of Ulster politics, they can rightfully expect
Unionists in turn to acknowledge the Ulster dimension of
politics in the Republic. Unionists must grant its full weight
to the fact that there has been no other occasion or cause
of political violence in the Republic since 1922 except
the partition of Ireland. To expect the Republic to treat
Northern Ireland as a "foreign state" is to condemn the
Republic, as well as Northern Ireland, to the threat of end-
lessly recurring violence. To expect politicians in the Republic
to "cease interfering" in the Northern problem is to expect
them to abdicate responsibility for maintaining peace and
safeguarding democracy within their own jurisdiction.
Northern Ireland is an internal and domestic problem in the
politics of the Irish Republic. Anyone who denies or ignores
that fact is running way from reality.

The politics of reconciliation

There are, I have argued, two Ulster loyalties, not one; two Ulster identities, not one. Yet, reconciliation, cooperation and partnership between these two loyalties and two identities is vitally and urgently needed, not only for the peace of both communities, but for the very survival of the civilised values of both the Northern Ireland traditions. We must no longer, as has sometimes happened even among Churchmen in the past, speak of reconciliation as if it were a matter of individuals or of person-to-person relations in special groups, even in reconciliation centres. These latter are indeed an essential element in reconciliation, and one could not praise too highly the courage and dedication of those who in the North have for many years been promoting centres and works of reconciliation of this kind. They have made an enormous contribution to over-all reconciliation. But reconciliation must also be between communities, and must involve the structures and institutions of society, as well as individuals and groups.

Nor must we, as sometimes even Churchmen have done, speak of reconciliation as though it were solely a moral and spiritual, as distinct from a political reality; or even as though it were a prior condition which had to be met before structures of justice could be created. Rather justice is an essential pre-requirement of reconciliation; indeed justice is itself an integral part of reconciliation. The historical and actual conflict in the North has been and is about power in all its forms, political, economic, social, cultural. It has been and is about wealth, privilege, opportunity, about jobs and prospects and promotion, about location of industry, about who controls what and who shares what. These are all questions of politics. They are questions of justice. Pope Paul, in his message for World Peace Day 1975, said:

> Peace can also lead to serious sacrifices. . . . It will even lead to the generosity of forgiveness and reconciliation: but never by way of abject betrayal of human dignity . . . never by way of baseness. Peace will never be without a hunger and thirst for justice . . .

We have for too long been afflicted in Northern Ireland by the restrictive and exclusivist mentality which says: "There are too few jobs; let's keep the few we have for our own."

The need in the 1970s is to say on the contrary: "We have too little talent or skill in our small province for us to be able to do without any that is available, from whichever side it comes. We have so few with leadership quality in our two communities that we cannot afford to exclude either from access to all forms of service for the good of both." The two communities in partnership and co-responsibility could make Northern Ireland a spiritually and culturally richer place, as well as a more prosperous and progressive economy than either community or either tradition alone could ever make it. Continued violence is nothing but a bilateral suicide pact. Partnership alone can give us a "life before death".

But for far too long in Northern Ireland we have wanted to predetermine the future for all time. We have refused validity of any future but that of our own particular political persuasion. We have denied legality to any future except that of Unionist *status quo* or republican aspiration as the case may be. We must learn to live with one another in the present and leave the future open. 1979 is not 1912 nor is it 1916, neither is it 2004. The men of the future will look after the future, provided we look after the present. We will look after the present by being faithful to the truth and the right as we see them, but allowing and actually wanting others to be faithful to the truth and the right as they see them. Those who seek to foreclose and predetermine the future only reveal that they are unsure of themselves and of the truth and rightness of their cause in the present. Those who seek a foreclosed future will not even have a livable present.

One is always conscious, when speaking about the Northern problem, of the inadequacy of words, the impotence of appeals to reason and to morality. Yet to despair of reason and of morality is to despair of man and even in part to cease to be human. He who believes in God can never despair of man. He faces the future with hope because God is our future.

Christian politicians will work with all the more urgency when they realise that ultimately peace is God's gift, and that the world with all its wisdom and experience cannot give it. It is God's gift — but to men of goodwill; and goodwill presupposes man's intelligence, integrity, energy and commitment. Peace, with the justice which is its condition, is a politician's most ultimate and categorical imperative. Only when the politician has done all that he can and more than he can for peace with justice, has he demonstrated the goodwill which deserves God's gift of peace.

We must all of us demonstrate this goodwill by the seriousness and unconditionality and unambiguousness of our renunciation of violence; by the private and public demonstration of our demand for peace; by the intensity of our perseverance in prayer. God must act in this situation, if peace is to come; but God can act only if we want him to and allow him to act. Prayer is the condition of God's all-powerful action for peace. Our prayer is indeed part of God's action for peace. It shares in the power of God's action. Prayer is part of God's omnipotent creation of the world. Prayer is part of God's power to make all things new.

Prayer is tested and proven by sacrifice. We must be prepared to suffer for peace, to take risks for peace — to suffer criticism, opposition, unpopularity for peace. Patrick Kavanagh wrote a moving little poem, "The Road to Hate":

He said: The road you are going will lead you to Hate
            For I went down that way yesterday and saw it away
            In the hollow a mile distant and I turned back
            Glad of my escape.

But I said: I will persist,
            For I know a man who went down the hill into the hollow
            and entered the very city of Hate
            And God visited him every day out of pity
            Till in the end he became a most noble saint.

Christ did more. He smuggled, not bombs and arms, but love and peace, forgiveness and reconciliation into mankind's City of Hate. And they crucified him for it. But that is how he became our peace. As St Paul said:

He is the peace between us, and has made the two into one and broken down the barrier which used to keep them apart, actually destroying in his own person the hostility (*Ephesians* 2:13-14).

The true Christians and the true patriots in Ireland today are those who set themselves to continue that reconciling work of Christ in our divided Irish communities.

3

VIOLENCE AND THE LIE

In an earlier book, *Violence in Ireland and Christian Conscience* (Veritas Publications, Dublin, 1973), I suggested the need for the "demythologising of revolutionary violence". But this process has to begin within ourselves and within our own emotions. It is in our own selves, sometimes against our own selves, that the struggle for peace has first to be waged. It begins with a struggle against the plausibility which the lie of violence has come to assume in our own half-conscious thinking, attitudes and emotions. We can and we do easily adopt cynical attitudes towards the possibility of peace. We can be brainwashed into believing that violence "works", "produces results", whereas politics is, on the contrary, evasive and suspect and peace is complacent, servile and utopian. I fear that we can all of us recognise that, at one time or another in our lives, in one degree of another, we have ourselves shared this attitude. Pope Paul, in his message for World Peace Day, 1974, identified this as one of the major obstacles to the achievement of peace. He said:

> Basically, what compromises the stability of peace and the movement of history in its favour is the unspoken and sceptical conviction that, in practice, peace is impossible. . . . There returns once again to men's minds . . . the thought that what matters is force . . .

Pope Paul roundly declared:

> To regard struggle among men as a structural need of society is not only an error of philosophy and vision but also a potential and permanent crime against humanity. . . . Modern man must have the moral and prophetic courage . . . (to regard) peace as something essentially natural, necessary, obligatory and therefore possible. We must henceforth consider humanity, history, work, politics, culture and progress in terms of their relationship to peace.

In so far as any of us may, at one time or another, as a result of a certain reading of world history or of Irish history, or as a result of frustration with the lack of political movement in the North, have come to regard violence as the "only solution" or as more effective than non-violent methods of reform, then Pope Paul's words are meant for us. They rebuke us. They call for a radical change of mentality. Pope Paul did not use words lightly. When he said "crime against humanity", he meant precisely what he said. These grave words call for earnest reflection and self-examination on the part of all of us.

The alternative, the moral and Christian challenge, which the Pope put before us is to believe, sincerely and strongly to believe, that peace is possible.

> Peace is possible, if each of us wants it; if each of us loves peace, educates and forms his own outlook to peace, defends peace, works for peace. Each one of us must listen in his own conscience to the impelling call: "Peace depends on you too."

In Ireland we have a particularly urgent need to take this message to ourselves. We must try to free ourselves from this spurious magic of the word violence. We must not think of peace as a negative thing, much less as a weak and servile thing. True peace is the positive activity of creating an order of justice. It is the active building of such structures and guarantees of equal justice for all that recourse to violence will be unnecessary and will be universally agreed to be both unnecessary and wrong. Peace is strong, with the very strength of God. Peace calls for courage, courage to stand with Christ against the bullying and brutality of violence. It is from the Cross of Christ that peace receives its meaning and its power. It was with his hands still gashed and red with the marks of the nails that the risen Christ said to his disciples: "Peace be with you." Peace is God's mighty work of reconciliation, generated by Christ's Passion, and released by Christ's Resurrection into the history of men.

We must work with determination to remove from ourselves and from our youth the false belief that violence is a proof of strength. It is peace which is strong. It is peace which is brave. It is peace which has the power to give both life and *lebensraum* in the true sense of space for a more human way of living. But to deserve peace and to have peace, we must work the works of justice. We must do justice to all men and try to ensure that justice to all is done in our society; and we must do this because God is just, because God is the vindicator of justice for all men, and not just because we are weary of war. The words "for peace's sake" have sometimes been given an unfavourable sense. We must instead give them a positive and noble sense. We must do right for the sake of peace, which is the product of justice and the means to justice. We must build peace for justice's sake.

Emotive and descriptive language

The well-known philosophical distinction between the emotive and the descriptive uses or "meanings" of words is relevant for the analysis of the lie surrounding violence. Words describe certain objects, situations or events. They also evoke certain emotions, suggest certain attitudes, favourable or unfavourable. The potent and sometimes dangerous magic of words is that they can change their descriptive meaning without losing their emotive power. Consequently, favourable or unfavourable emotions can be re-directed towards different objects by continuing to repeat a familiar word with established emotive power, but gradually altering its descriptive reference, or substituting a new referent (which is a convenient term for the object referred to). Much of the technique, and much of the success, of modern advertising depends upon this phenomenon. Propaganda in every sphere depends upon it. It is enlightening to try to detect the operation of this process in the media.

In the political sphere, much of the propaganda of Nazism was based upon expert exploitation of this technique. Much of the propaganda of communism deploys it very successfully; to the extent of having substituted new descriptive content for the whole range of words associated with "democratic", "popular", "people's", even "free" and "freedom", while retaining the aura of emotional satisfaction and enthusiasm which these words had come to acquire in earlier stages of history, when their descriptive meaning was quite different. It must be added, of course, that capitalism has been successful in practising similar propaganda exercises.

In our own country, the abuse is vividly exemplified in the propaganda of the so-called "republican movement". The term "Republic", and all the associated words have, throughout Western history, had a strong emotive appeal. In Irish history, particularly in recent centuries, the words enshrine a noble tradition, embodying much of what is most cherished in the aspirations, dreams and hopes of a people struggling to be free from ancient bondage. The words recall much of what is noblest in our island history. The very use of these terms is enough by itself to evoke a spontaneous approving and supportive response.

If, however, a group of men can arrogate to themselves the use of these emotive terms, they can confuse some people to the extent of tricking them into approving, or at least condoning and excusing, their policies and practices — even when those policies are the repudiation of everything the traditional republican movement stood for, and even though their practices bring disgrace and dishonour upon an honourable tradition. There is no historical continuity whatever between the present, largely faceless, leaders of the self-styled "republican movement" and their honourable forbears; there is no moral continuity between their methods and those of the earlier struggle for independence. One of the aims of the present "republican movement" is to overthrow the very institutions of democracy which earlier republicans sacrificed limb and life to establish. The means which present republicans are using are predominantly means which are directly contradictory of the prayer of the Republican Proclamation of Easter Monday, 1916, "that no one who serves that cause will dishonour it by . . . inhumanity . . ." In short, the present "republican movement" has nothing but the name in common with the earlier tradition described by that title. The term now has a totally different content, an utterly new referent: it describes different leaders, different men, different methods, different concepts of liberation, different moralities and codes of revolutionary way. Yet the magic of the name "republican movement" continues to exert its fatal fascination. The term can still evoke the emotions which stirred earlier generations; and those hypnotised by them are scarcely conscious that it is to something utterly new and alien and ugly and evil to which they are now giving their emotional sympathy or support.

On the other side of our tragic community divide, the abuse by loyalist terrorists of the honoured name of Protestant is, if anything, more repellent still. For many Irishmen, the term Protestant stands for what is most noble, most precious and most sacred and holy in their lives and their reasons for living. We extend our sympathy towards them for the pain they suffer when they read of crimes of horror and shame committed by people claiming to be Protestant and claiming to be defending Protestantism. One of the more unfortunate features of our present tragic situation is that, partly because of this emotive abuse of words, the misdeeds of a few come to be regarded as typical of the many. But the crimes of loyalist terrorists, bombers and assassins have no more to do with Protestantism than the crimes of their republican counterparts have to do with Catholicism. This is why Church leaders have been so anxious to insist that the inter-community violence in Northern Ireland is not a "religious war". The Churches must not be made the scapegoat for decades, even generations, of political neglect and chicanery. The Churches cannot be expected to solve, in face of the obstruction of politicians, problems created and sustained by politicians.

The Church can and must and will continue to proclaim God's law. But those who, in the case in question, are violating that law are not there to hear. It is ironic to reflect that, according to probable estimates, in the sectors of Belfast usually referred to as "Protestant areas"and regarded as the "Protestant heart-land", probably scarcely five per cent of the population are practising Christians. Could there be a more glaring example of the contrast between the descriptive and the emotive use of the term "Protestant"? The term has retained the emotive resonance which it deserves, so long as it is used to describe a religious faith and a Christian way of life. But it has come to describe instead a set of fears, suspicions, passions, prejudices, characteristic of colonialism, racialism, tribalism; and, more positively, ex-colonialist insecurity, lack of economic and social confidence, lack of trust in their neighbours in either island, and absence of national identity.

The case of republican militants vis-à-vis Catholic affiliation is similar. They reserve an area of their lives and behaviour — that area precisely which defines them as republicans — over which God's law does not apply. For this area they have written for themselves a revised version of the divine law. To that extent, they have made their republican ideology into a god-substitute; and its slogans are their god-words. Of how many fanatical republicans could we not use the biblical words: "There be your gods, oh Israel." Here is another glaring example of the potency and danger of the emotive use of words.

In our society, and at a stage in our country's history when slogan-borne emotion has such a fateful influence over behaviour, it is vital that we unmask the slogans, look hard at the underlying realities, and refuse to be duped by the persuasive re-definitions. Davis said: "Educate that you may be free." Unless we become educated in making reason prevail over emotion in our use of words, we could, more easily and more quickly than we realise, lose the freedom which Ireland has so recently achieved, after so long a struggle, and at such a cost.

The masks of violence

One of those who has unmasked the face of contemporary violence and eloquently exposed its lie is Alexander Solzhenitsyn. In his Nobel speech on literature, in 1970, Solzhenitsyn said:

> This twentiety century of ours has proved crueller than the preceding ones, nor did all its terrors end with its first fifty years. . . . The primitive refusal to compromise has been elevated to the status of a theoretical principle: it is considered the virtue of orthodoxy. This refusal to compromise claims millions of victims in eternal internecine wars, tediously hammering home its message that there is no stable, universal human conception of goodness and justice, but all such conceptions are fluid and changeable, so that you should always act to the advantage of your own party. The extent of the violence that swings to and fro within Western society — or so it seems to an onlooker from without — is so great that the stage must surely be reached when the system will become unstable and must collapse. Violence, less and less restrained by the legal system built

up over the centuries, strides bold and victorious through the world, caring not a jot that its sterility has been amply demonstrated and proven throughout history.

The ruthless logic of violence

We are witnessing in our time the emergence of a philosophy and a methodology and a practice of total revolutionary violence, which correspond exactly to the evil philosophy of total war and which are equally intrinsically immoral. There is in revolutionary violence an escalator of viciousness, a kind of desperation of ruthlessness, which irresistibly impels towards more and more brutal excesses, more and more implacable killings. Moral limits are removed one after the other. Deeds that first seemed unthinkable become thought of as possible, then decided to be necessary, then remorselessly done. Earlier rather than later in the campaign, something gets killed in the killers: it is compassion, it is pity, it is conscience, it is humanity. Once the momentum of violence is set in motion, its moving staircase of fanatical logic takes over and becomes almost impossible to stop.

It is difficult not to suppose that some of those involved in the campaigns of violence, whether "republican" or "loyalist", when they compare their moral judgements now with those they would have made at the beginning of the campaign, might scarcely recognise themselves as the men who started out with certain ideals, certain hopes, certain principles. One can only hope and pray that they may, in some calm moment, silence the sound of the patriotic songs, the emotional speeches, the seductive slogans, and let the voice of conscience, the voice of God, have a chance to be heard in the silence. Certainly, we who look helplessly on, cannot but remember the words of Yeats:

> Things fall apart; the centre cannot hold;
> Mere anarchy is loosed upon the world,
> The blood-dimmed tide is loosed, and everywhere
> The ceremony of innocence is drowned;
> The best lack all conviction, while the worst
> Are full of passionate intensity.
>
> *The Second Coming*

It was of 1919 that Yeats wrote:

> We pieced our thoughts into philosophy,
> And planned to bring the world under a rule,
> Who are but weasels fighting in a hole
>
> . . . .
> We, who seven years ago
> Talked of honour and of truth,
> Shriek with pleasure if we show
> The weasel's twist, the weasel's tooth.

The words are shatteringly relevant for us, as we look almost despairingly back on ten years of violence.

Violence and the lie

These are the ugly facts of violence. They are masked by the emotive slogans. Solzhenitsyn, if I may quote him again, says in the same speech:

> Let us not forget that violence does not exist alone and cannot survive in isolation: it is inevitably bound up with the lie.
>
> Between them there is the most intimate, most natural, fundamental link; violence can only be concealed by the lie, and the lie can be maintained only by violence. Any one who has once proclaimed that violence is his method is inevitably forced to choose the lie as his guiding principle. At its birth violence acts openly, is even proud of itself. But it has scarcely established itself when it feels the air around it becoming more rarefied, and it cannot continue to exist without masking itself with a lie and wrapping itself up in its honeyed rhetoric. Violence does not always necessarily take you physically by the throat and strangle you: more often it merely demands of its subjects that they declare allegiance to the lie, become accomplices in the lie.

Solzhenitsyn sees the struggle against violence as being essentially the struggle against the lying propaganda of violence. In this struggle, he assigns the leading responsibility to the writers and artists. Their help is certainly needed in our country at this time. They, together with historians, sociologists, community workers, have a vital role to play, and many have already made a distinguished contribution. All these, together with politicians on the one hand and theologians, pastors, catechists and educators generally, on the other, must collaborate in trying to ensure that, for future generations, a lie that has long bewitched our own country, distorted our own history, and, too often, perverted our Christianity, will be at last eliminated. All those involved in influencing opinion and forming the young must endeavour to deepen our imaginative insight, improve our rational analysis, enlighten our conscience, above all stress the social and political dimensions of Christian conscience and raise the level of honesty and effectiveness in our political thinking and action, so that we can morally repudiate violence, without incurring the moral guilt of condoning the injustice that often occasions violent revolution. The true men of peace are those who are inbued, as much as, indeed more than. any militant, by the moral passion for justice which often provided the first motivation for revolutionary violence.

The legitimate line of succession from the republican freedom fighters of sixty years ago, the true continuity of the historic republican movement, is not found in the military struggle of today. It belongs to the men who are working peacefully and constructively for the economic and social and human development of this entire island. In this Republic of ours, the best republicans are those who are working non-violently for a just society in which all Irishmen can strive together for the common good of all our people.

We must pray as we work for that justice which is the only true basis for peace; we must work as we pray to remove the injustices in society from which violence usually and almost inevitably springs. As we pray every day, at the end of the Lord's Prayer, "deliver us from evil", let us ask especially that the Lord deliver us from the evil of violence and the hate and bitterness which it engenders. Let us pray that we may be set free from the grip of the lie surrounding violence. As Solzhenitsyn puts it:

> Once the lie has been dispersed, the nakedness of violence will be revealed in all its repulsiveness, and then violence, becoming decrepit, will come crashing down.

Solzhenitsyn ends his remarkable speech by saying:

> *One word of truth outweighs the whole world.* And on such a fantastic breach of the law of conservation of mass and energy are based my own activties and my appeal to the writers of the world.

Christians have the highest and noblest of all words of truth.
Our hopes, our certitude of the victory of peace, are founded
on the Word that made and truly outweighs the world, the
word of him who said:

> You will learn the truth
> and the truth will make you free . . .
> I am the Way, the Truth and the Life (*John* 8:32; 14:16).

PEACE TO ST PATRICK'S SONS

The words and example of St Patrick can help us to come to grips with the Gospel of Christ and to apply it fearlessly to ourselves and our situation in the Ireland of the end of the 1970s. His message is a summons to renewal and reconciliation. There is no renewal without some cutting off and rejection of the dead, outmoded past. We must cut off and burn the dead sprigs if new shoots are to grow. We must, St Paul says, "get rid of all the old yeast of evil and wickedness", is we are to have the "completely new batch of bread" . . . (made of) "sincerity and truth" (1 *Corinthians* 5:7-8). The process is painful. It has to be thorough-going, it has got to hurt, if real newness of healthy life and growth is to result. Reconciliation is a putting into one whole again of broken pieces, broken bones; it is getting opposites to fit together; it is getting opponents to shake hands. This too is painful. Broken bones hurt when they begin to knit. Broken pride and prejudice wince when brought into the same company with their hate-objects. But unless fractures are healed, there is no way forward. There is no other way to walk at all. Without reconciliation, there is no way to survive, no way to live, in Ireland in 1979.

A few days before St Patrick's Day five years ago, a young man was shot dead in a Belfast street, with a bullet fired at close range through his head. That young man was on his way home to his bed-ridden mother, with whom he lived as her constant help and support. She had had her leg amputated and could not move or turn in bed without her son's help. She waited for him that night to return and prepare her for sleep. As she was waiting, she could have heard the bullets. She never would have thought it could be her son; for he never failed to come home to her; he always came home at midnight. For once, he was late. She waited. But that night he did not come. He will not be coming again, ever.

That was Ireland, in the week of St Patrick five years ago. If we knew the circumstances, if we were a member of the family, a neighbour, a friend, we would know that each one of the two thousand dead of ten years of violence presented a comparable picture of personal tragedy, widowhood, orphanhood, nervous breakdown, desolation. What would St Patrick say of it? We do not have to speculate or invent. We know what he did say to men of violence who killed and terrorised Irish Christians in his own time. To the guerilla captain, Coroticus, who had raided the Irish coast from Wales sometime about 440 A.D., leaving death and mutilation and terror behind, Patrick wrote:

> I will not call them my fellow-citizens, but fellow-citizens of the demons, because of their evil works. . . . They live in death. . . . Dripping with blood, they welter in the blood of innocent Christians. . . . So let every God-fearing man know that they are enemies of me and of Christ my God, for whom I am an ambassador. Parricide! Fratricide! . . . What Christian would not shudder to be merry with such persons or to enjoy a meal with them? (St Patrick, *Letter to Coroticus*, 2, 5, 13).

And yet Patrick calls on them to repent and offers them the assurance of God's mercy if they "recover their senses", abandon their crimes and ask God's forgiveness. Every Catholic priest and Christian minister in Ireland must renew this plea to any of the men of violence who will listen to them at this time.

The men of loyalist violence will not be likely even to know about anything a Catholic bishop says. Would there be perhaps some possibility that some man of republican violence would hear, would listen? In any case, those who speak God's word, as we know from the Biblical prophets, are not bound to make men listen. They are bound to speak, whether men listen or whether they don't. In God's name, in Ireland's name, may some responsible Christian man in the republican movement listen.

Descent to gangsterism

The present campaign of violence, now in its tenth year, has turned into a very different campaign from the one its leaders may have foreseen or intended in 1969. It has different personnel, a different philosophy; it uses new and more vicious tactics; it has developed a new and perverse and utterly amoral ethic to justify these tactics. It relies more and more for its operations on teenage youngsters, girls as well as boys, who have been brainwashed from boyhood and from girlhood into unfeeling and remorseless disregard for human life, any murder or crime being held justifiable by the inhuman principle that all means are good to achieve a revolutionary end.

The descent into ruthlessness should have been foreseen. Everyone should have known that when God's law, "Thou shalt not kill", is violated, then no-one's life is any longer safe. The killing of girl prison officers; the shooting dead of fathers in the presence of wives and terrified children; the destruction by bombs of the hotel-residence of retired old people; the terrorising of the wives and children of "proxy" bomb-carriers or of car-owners or of bank managers; the shooting dead of a bank customer who happens to be in the way of a bank raider — such is the descent into barbarism which is the logical trajectory of modern terrorist violence.

It is said that in a campaign of violence it is a man's first killing that is repellent to him. After the first, the others follow with cold indifference. This is understandable. The first bullet or bomb does not only kill an opponent; it also kills part of the killer. The campaign has also evoked a barbaric kind of reaction, which should always have been foreseen, but which, in recent years, has been totally predictable and is wholly unavoidable every week the violence continues. The campaign has been a manifest source of manifold moral degeneracy, especially among youth. Its effects will be with us for decades, in the shape of warped personalities, crippled communities, social casualties and debased morals, not to speak of the two thousand dead and the maimed bodies and the mutilated lives of survivors and relatives.

The campaign gives every indication now of having no direction, no control, no rational purpose, no attainable aims, no foreseeable end. "Successes", in the shape of deaths inflicted, explosions effected, disruption brought about, are no proof to the contrary. Japan's death-defying warriors continued to have "successes" of precisely that kind, right up to the moment of capitulation.

Because of this campaign, whole areas of northern cities have sunk into conditions which could be compaed only to the gangster-land of Al Capone's Chicago or to the seamy blood-feuds of the Mafia. There is in whole areas of the North a régime of lawless gun-law, which rivals the fictional Wild West; only there is no idealism, no glamour, no respect for the weak and old and innocent, no reward for virtue, nothing but scorn, contempt and abuse for those who abhor killing and desire peace.

Appeal to leaders

Probably no greater factor of de-Christianisation is at present at work in Ireland than the continuing violence. Do its leaders want to go down in history as the people who played a major part in hastening the decline of Christianity in our country, fifteen hundred years after St Patrick?

Probably no campaign waged by Irishmen ever resorted to such persistently vicious tactics as that now wrecking the North. The 1916 leaders prayed that no-one who served the Republic might "dishonour it by . . . inhumanity or rapine". Do the present leaders of republican violence want to be the men who dishonour the Republic by condoning the inhumanity, intimidation and cold-blooded murders now being practised in its name?

Republicanism, once a proud and honoured name, is being dragged in the gutter, made a synonym of shame. Do the republican leaders realise that, because of what is being done in the North, some people are being given the excuse to belittle Irish history, decry nationalism and patriotism as such, apologise for Irishness. Do they want to be the people who will provide a pretext for some to turn to any form of vulgar cosmo-provincialism or genteel West Britonism, on the argument that they wish to espouse the direct cultural opposite of the republicanism whose ugly face they have seen in the North. Men of an older and nobler republican tradition should raise their voices to protest against what is being done today to besmirch its name. Honourable and responsible men in the present republican leadership should stop now before all decency has leaked away and there is no honour left to save.

No imaginable benefit to a future Ireland could justify this campaign. A future Ireland is in fact being shaped by the campaign itself; and it would be an Ireland which no dead Irish patriot would recognise and with which no living patriot would want to identify. No greater service could be rendered to Ireland at this time by any Irishman than would be rendered to her by the republican leader who would now have the courage to say to his colleagues: "This is enough. This must stop."

To do so will not be to admit defeat and be guilty of betrayal or failure. It will be yielding to the code of honour which has always motivated patriots. It will be not defeat but victory, victory for humanity, for realism, for reason, for pride in Ireland's past, for hope of Ireland's future. It will be victory for past republicanism's record in the annals of freedom, for Ireland's present respect among the nations of the world. Cowardice and conformism among the leaders will only let the situation slide further and further out of any leader's control into aimless terror. Courage on the part of even one leader, the rare courage of one who can stand in the right even if he stands alone, could save the movement from irreparable disgrace at the bar of history.

The Christian and judgement

But we all have a responsibility as Christians in the face of this situation. Our responsibility is one with our response to the words of Christ in the Gospel. St Patrick summons us all to return to the source of our faith in God's Word in the Bible. Cardinal Newman said, and the words are relevant for this Holy Year:

Contemplate the picture (of the Gospel). Do not shut your eyes, do not revolt from it, do not fret under it, but look at it. Bear to look at the Christianity of the Bible; bear to contemplate the idea of the Christian, traced by God's inspiration, without gloss, or comment, or tradition of man. Bear to hear read to you a number

of texts . . . which are no partial selections, but a specimen of the
whole of the New Testament. . . . Realise the idea of the Scriptural
Christian. . . . Study what the Bible Christian is; be silent over it;
pray for grace to comprehend it, to accept it (*Sermons on Subjects
of the Day*, 289-290).

There are many sentences in the Gospel which could have
been spoken of our situation in the North. What I should say
is that there are many sentences which are being spoken by
Christ now to our situation in the North. Let me refer to
one or two.

Christ said: "Do not judge, and you will not be judged"
(*Matthew* 7:1). He said: "If there is one of you who has not
sinned, let him be the first to throw a stone" (*John* 7:7). If
we could take that to heart and cease to judge *others* but
begin to realise that it is *we* who are under judgement, we
would be much closer to a solution and an end. It is un-
Christian to judge whole communities because of the crimes
of a few. It is un-Christian if Catholics say: "This is all so
typical of Protestants: they are all black bigots, deep down."
It is un-Christian if Protestants say: "This is all so typical of
Catholics: they were always treacherous at heart; it is the
way they are educated and indoctrinated by their priests and
their Church." It is un-Christian if anyone in the Republic
says: "This is so typical of Northerners: they are all intolerant,
and one side is as bad as the other; let them fight it out
between them and leave us alone in peace." It is un-Christian
if Englishmen say: "This is so typical of Irishmen: they are
an impossible lot; let them fight it out among them and let us
get on with our own problems in peace."

These terrible deeds we deplore in the North are not
"typical of Protestants". Many of those who commit them
probably never entered a Protestant church, or heard a
Protestant sermon or met a Protestant clergyman. These
deeds are abhorred and detested by all "typical" Protestants;
for "typical" Protestants are God-fearing and neighbour-
loving Christians, men of charity, integrity, honesty and
courage. "Typical" Protestants are our allies in the present
and future struggle to keep Ireland Christian.

The terrible deeds we deplore in the North are not "typical
of Catholics". They are a violation of every principle of
Catholic morality, a contradiction of every sermon preached

by Catholic priests in every pulpit in Catholic churches all over the North for the past ten years. They are a defiance of the teaching of every Catholic bishop. They are a rejection of everything taught in Catholic schools. "Typical" Catholics abhor them. Whenever Catholics have had a democratic opportunity to do so, they have publicly repudiated them and have shown that they want no part of them.

These terrible deeds are not "typical of Northeners". The "typical Northener" is one of the finest types of Irishmen; and throughout these terrible years, whether Catholic or Protestant, he has shown a courage, a resilience, a good-humoured and unselfconscious imperturbability, which will receive proper recognition in the future and which will yet provide an inspiration for all Ireland. A "typical Northener" wrote:

> We men of the North had a word to say
> and we said it then in our own dour way
> and we spoke out loud and clear.

But the "dour way" the Northener speaks — and I know it, having spent all my early life in settings of absolutely typical Protestant-Catholic good-neighbourliness, first in a rural and then in an urban environment — the "dour way" the Northener speaks, I repeat, is a way of kindness, neighbourliness, loyal friendship, decency and dependability.

These terrible deeds are not "typical of Irishmen". Much of the responsibility for the historic situation which led up to them, even in the less remote past, lies with successive Parliaments and Governments at Westminster. Those who throw moral stones only break their own squinting windows. The problem of urban violence is one which every modern society will have to face and for which no modern society has found the answer. As Britain, or our own Republic, come increasingly to have to cope with it, there will be no room for smugness about the North.

Failure of Christianity?

It is inconsequent for the critic of Christianity or the Churches to say: "These terrible deeds are typical consequences of Christianity. They show the failure of religion, the failure of the Churches." The Churches have no power to prevent people using the Protestant or the Catholic name, even when they are doing things that are the very contradiction of Protestantism or Catholicism. How in reason can the Protestant Churches be held responsible for what happens in urban areas, where perhaps as few as five per cent of the population are church-going? How in justice can the Catholic Church be blamed for not being listened to by people who have been indoctrinated into contempt and defiance of every tenet of their Church regarding the morality of their violent deeds? What can Christians do but "proclaim the message and, welcome or unwelcome, insist on it; refute falsehood, correct error, call to obedience" (*2 Timothy* 4:1-2). Call to obedience we must; but we cannot enforce obedience. The Gospel coerces indeed, but only by conviction, only through conversion of the heart. Human coercion is no part of the preaching of the Gospel. The Gospel judges. God judges men by the Gospel. But the Christian must not judge and dare not coerce.

Our complicity

The terrible deeds of the North place us all under the judgement of God. Let us listen to St James:

> Where do these wars and battles between yourselves first start? Isn't it precisely in the desires fighting inside your own selves? You want something and you haven't got it; so you are prepared to kill. You have an ambition that you cannot satisfy; so you fight to get your way by force (*James* 4:1-2).

The very same passions which are erupting in bombs, bullets and blood in the North are fighting inside our own selves. The passions which are at work in the North are at work in our society and in our lives too, though they take different forms. Hatred, ruthlessness, abuse of power; the make-a-profit-quick mentality, the take-any-advantage-you-can-get-away-with philosophy, the grab-a-sexual-thrill-when-you-can ethic, these are all simply aliases for violence. They are simply different names for the Seven Deadly Sins, which are all the more deadly when we forget their proper names and therefore do not recognise their presence.

The violent passions at work in our own lives deprive us of any right to feel superior about the violence which is wrecking the North. The adjunction of Christ not to judge others

carries with it the warning to judge ourselves. It is to us that
Christ says: "Unless you repent, you will all perish as they
did. (*Luke* 13:3). The present is a time for recognising and
admitting our sinfulness and our complicity with all who sin.
That is the beginning of all liberation; that is the first step to
renewal and to reconciliation. May God give us the courage,
the honesty and strength to do it. May God have mercy on us
and take pity on our country.

Protestant Irish and Catholic Irish in the United States

St Patrick is honoured by Irishmen across the whole world.
He is honoured by Protestant Irish as much as by Catholic
Irish, in the United States, in Canada, in Australia, in New
Zealand, in South Africa. When Irish people leave their homeland, they rapidly discover a common Irishness and − to
quote Yeats − the "much hatred" sometimes engendered by
the "little room" of our island seems suddenly irrelevant in
the broader spaces overseas. We must try to create these
broader spaces in the mind and the spirit, so that much love
may flourish where hatred now grows rank.

It is inspiring for sons of St Patrick at home to recall how
two Irish traditions met and converged in the founding and
the prospering of the American Republic, which recently
celebrated its bicentennial − the Catholic Irish tradition and
the Protestant Irish tradition. The significant thing to recall
now is that people of both these traditions came to America
out of a common desire for freedom, a common detestation
of tyranny and injustice, a common determination to create
here a new nation of equality, tolerance and justice. The
Ulster Protestant Irish who came, mainly Presbyterian in
stock, were, as one of their historians, R. J. Dickson, has
remarked, smarting under "the badge of inferiority" in their
homeland. "Their ardour in the Revolution", the same
historian observes, "was a thanksgiving to a land which had
received them in their distress."

In this common dedication of two Irish traditions to the
creation and the building up of the free Republic of America,
I see hope for Ireland today. The same two Irish traditions
must now join together again, to create a new and just and
tolerant and truly democratic society in their island homeland.

A great Irish and American patriot, Thomas D'Arcy McGee, delivered a speech in Montreal in 1861 on what he called "The Policy of Conciliation". In it he said that:

With men of different origins and cultures, if we do not bear and forbear, if we do not get rid of old quarrels, but, on the contrary make fresh ones . . . ; if each neighbour will try, not only to nurse old animosities, but to invent new ground of hostility, then we shall return to what Hobbes called the state of nature (in which the life of man is mean, poor, nasty, brutish and short) . . .

In society we must sacrifice something. We must sometimes make way for men like ourselves, though we could prove by the most faultless syllogism our right to push them from the path.

D'Arcy McGee's "policy of conciliation" is the way to peace; it is the only way to peace with justice, freedom with law, in Ireland. Partnership is what Ireland needs, not polarisation; sharing of responsibility between the two communities and not suppression or coercion of either; a policy of conciliation, not a policy of mutual self-destruction.

May both historic communities in Ireland, the Protestant and the Catholic, come to recognise this. May we both recognise what President Kennedy called "our indivisibility as children of God and our common vulnerability on this planet"; we would say, in our Irish context, "our common vulnerability on this island". What Protestant Irishmen and Catholic Irishmen were able to do together in America in 1776 and to build together in the two hundred year history of the United States, they can do together and build together in Ireland in 1979.

It was the hope of an Irish Presbyterian who wrote, in his *History of Presbyterianism,* in 1910:

May the time soon come when Irishmen of all creeds and classes, forgetting the bitter memories of the past or thinking of these only to learn the wisdom of a better course, shall work together for the common good of our beloved land.

There could be no better way for Irishmen of all denominations and persuasions to prove themselves true sons of St Patrick. St Patrick spoke to the men of violence in his time:

May God inspire them sometime to recover their senses for God, repenting, however late, their heinous deeds . . . in order that they may deserve to live with God, and be made whole, here and in eternity. Be peace to the Father, and to the Son, and to the Holy Spirit. Amen. (*Letter to Coroticus,* transl. by Ludwig Bieler, 21).

BLESSED ARE THE PEACEMAKERS

The beatitudes represent the greatest reversal of earthly values ever seen in the history of morals. They constitute a "transvaluation of values", compared to which Nietzche's can only be called romantic if not degenerate rhetoric. The beatitudes have been said to represent "the kind of thing which tends to happen to a group of people when the Kingdom of God breaks through". They are a statement of the spirit which should animate a community and a people who try to live by the Gospel of Christ. It is a valuable exercise to compare the beatitudes, one by one, with the picture of the good life which is widely diffused through modern Western secular society. Much of contemporary secular society operates on principles which are diametrically opposed to the beatitudes and to the principles of the Gospel. This is not to say that modern society is totally degenerate. It is only to say that it needs to be redeemed. St Paul knew, in his time, a not too dissimilar society, and he said about it: "This may be a wicked age, but your lives should redeem it." Our society, scarred by many of the wounds of wickedness, will not be redeemed without the Cross.

The shadow of the Cross falls over all the beatitudes. Their blessedness is worlds apart from what the adman calls bliss. The price of the world's peace was paid in blood on the Cross. To cut violence out of the body of humanity is major surgery. The first incisions were made by the nails which ripped through the wrists and ankles of Christ on the Cross. That operation was without anaesthetics. It is not for nothing that St Matthew groups the blessing of the peacemakers with the blessing of those persecuted in the cause of right. The blessing which is in question in all the beatitudes is that of belonging to the Kingdom of him whom the Irish call "the King of

Friday". The blessed are "the King of Friday's men".

The beatitudes are not primarily descriptions of states of soul or exhortations to cultivate certain moral virtues or spiritual attitudes. They are primarily statements of the nature of God's Kingdom. They tell us what the Kingdom is about. It is inherent in the nature of the Kingdom that the poor and the gentle and the suffering and the hungry, the despised, the oppressed and the persecuted should be part of it. The Kingdom is about the reconciliation of enmities, the ending of hostilities and the building of peace — and that is why the peacemakers belong to it.

Christ's work in the world is essentially peace-making — making peace between men and God and between man and man. St Paul puts it graphically:

> In Christ Jesus, you that used be so far apart have been brought very close, by the blood of Christ. For he is the peace between us and has made the two into one and broken down the barrier which used to keep them apart, actively destroying in his own person the hostility caused by . . . the Law . . . In his own person (Christ) killed the hostility (*Ephesians* 2:16).

There could be not greater barrier between human groups than that of which St Paul was speaking, the barrier between Jews and pagans. It was religious, moral, racial, cultural. But the Church broke down the barrier and made both groups one in Christ.

Christ himself frequently gave the example of Jews and Samaritans as typical of the kind of reconcilitation he came to bring about. Everybody knew, as St John drily remarked, that "Jews do not associate with Samaritans". It was a moral virtue and a religious duty in the minds of pious Jews to shun Samaritans. But Jesus went out of his way to talk with them, to mix with them, to hold them up as an example to the Jews. "In his own person he killed the hostility." But he was killed for it himself. He took the full fury of man's hostility upon himself until it killed him. The gashes of the wounds were still red and raw in his hands and feet and side before he was able to give the peace he had promised and to say: "Peace be with you."

Killing hate

As Jesus was hanging on the Cross, some of those near him heard him cry out: "Father, forgive them; they do not know what they are doing." That is where the victory over hates lies: defeating haters by forgiveness.

The executioners knew very well, of course, what they were doing; every bit as well as our killers and haters know what they are doing in our day. But Jesus did not come to judge such men, but to save them; to save them from themselves, their passions, their vengeances and their hates. Christ took the cutting whiplash of human hatred on his bare bent back, without a word; and he killed it. He killed it, not by retaliation and revenge, but by forgiving it.

Christ will have nothing of the "tit for tat", "ten of theirs for five of ours", mentality. By such policies one does not kill hate; one only spreads it. By such policies one only offers hate new victims, new lives for poisoning, new personalities for warping. There is only one way to destroy hatred; and that is by refusing to let it get into one's life and corrupt one's personality. That is what stops hatred in its tracks. That is what says "no way" to hate. Nothing else does. By any other way, hate wins; and we are all losers.

This was how Christ beat hate. He took the blows of hate right on the heart, and he killed it. He "killed the hostility in his own person" – by forgiving it. Christ said once that it is what comes out of the heart that counts. Out of Christ's pierced heart came only forgiveness and reconciliation, love and new life.

Christians must know that this, and only this, is the way to victory over hate. They know this, and only this, does and will triumph. They know that this is as sure as Christ rose from the dead. They know it, because hate can only kill, it cannot give life. When hate had finished with killing Christ, it had never even touched the love which was his life. Out of the dead he rose. He spoke. And what he said was, *Peace*. He lives again. He has the last word. It is true: "Love one another; forgive one another; be reconciled."

Because of Christ, we have a future. One must abandon hopelessness, if one believes in Christ. Christ is our future – the Lamb who was killed by hate, yet lives by love, and will never die.

The violence within

It is only by a violent struggle against our own passions and emotions that we can kill the hostility in our persons. Most of us in these islands must humbly and sadly confess how far we are from having killed in ourselves the hostility of passion, prejudice and partnership, which is first cousin to the hostilities of guns and bullets. So many of us, through these bitter years, have been saying: "The other community began it; it is they who must stop it first." "The other side are ruthless terrorists; our side are only bravely defending themselves." "The people of the other island could never be trusted or respected; we are guiltless if only we were left alone." In the past five years, how many of us in Ireland and in Britain have been reproducing every classic guilt-evading prototype given in the Bible. Like Adam and Eve, we have each blamed the other and both blamed the devil. Like the Pharisee, we have thanked God publicly and eloquently that we were not like the rest of men: not like the exploiting British; not like the murderous Irish; not like the bigoted Irish Protestants; not like the uncouth Irish Catholics; not like the reactionary Church establishments. How many of us in both islands have played the Pilate, washing our hands of guilt or responsibility and saying: "I am innocent of this blood: it is your concern." The hostility is not killed, because we will not recognise it as our concern and kill it, each in his own person.

But many have not tired of working to build upon the bomb-sites and have not ceased to speak peace across the barricades. The tale of the Christian faith and love and hope and fortitude of priests and ministers, community leaders and ordinary men and women, from both communities, has yet to be told. In the case of most, it will never be told. Before we boast of our own superior tolerance or virtue or ecumenical spirit, let us humbly acknowledge that "we have not yet had to keep fighting to the point of death", as many of them have, "in the fight against sin". These men and women surely merit to hear from their Master the words: "Blessed are the peacemakers: they shall be called sons of God."

They have often taken their lives in their hands. It is characteristic of extremists on both sides, even when they propagandise about seeking a united community, to hate, intimidate and even kill those who work to reconcile the communities. But the peacemakers have not desisted. They were able, like the Master, to take the fury of violence on themselves, so as to destroy it in their own person.

All Christians are called to that work of the making of peace. The Eucharist gives us our daily and weekly mission to make peace. The mangled Body in which and through which human hate has been overcome, is "given up" for us in every Mass, so that we may give ourselves up to others, to all men, in the work of forgiveness, love and peace. "Go in peace" is not an end of Eucharistic worship so much as a beginning of Eucharistic life. From Mass we go to spread the peace we have been given. It is a peace the world did not give and cannot find. It is the peace given by the Risen Lord, who by dying has overcome the worst violence that hostility can wreak, and by rising from the dead has brought a peace which ultimately the world cannot destroy. There lies across the beatitudes the shadow of the Cross. But this shadow is cast by the Cross standing against the light of Easter. As the Irish have it, the King of Friday is also the King of Sunday; and his men are Sunday's men.

The conditions of moral condemnation

In the spirit of the beatitudes, we are certainly obliged to denounce and to condemn those who are at present committed in Ireland to enforcing political change by violent means. The same spirit of the beatitudes obliges us also, however, to be careful lest our moral condemnation take on some of the qualities of the very violence which is being denounced, or become tainted by traces of moral pharisaism.

I should like, in this connection, to distinguish between moral condemnation, on the one hand, and moralistic denunciation, on the other.

Moral condemnation is directed at the evil deed more directly than at the evildoer. It avoids verbal abuse or verbal violence directed at the sinner. It is predicated on the possibility and the hope of his change of heart, and carries with it the promise of forgiveness and reconciliation. It tries to understand the circumstances and the motives which have lead the evildoer to do evil acts; and by understanding them hopes to transform the circumstances and to correct the motives. It accepts the speaker's share of guilt for the circumstances in which evil is done. The condemnation is uttered in awareness of one's own need for repentance and forgiveness. To have the right to utter moral condemnation, one must recognise one's own sinfulness; indeed one's own capacity for sinning in the precise ways one is condemning. Simultaneously with expressing condemnation of evil, one must be recognising one's own need to be forgiven.

Moral condemnation is therefore something one does sadly rather than jubilantly, hesitantly rather than over-readily. The sadness comes both from the recollection of one's own guilt, and also from one's regret that men and women who are called to share God's life and love, and who are capable of so much goodness, should instead be perpetrating deeds of murder and injustice, hatred and cruelty.

Moral condemnation tries to be deliberately conscious of the risks which attend condemning others — especially the Pharisee's risk of "thanking God that we are not as the rest of men". The Christian can never forget the solemn words of Christ: "Judge not that you may not be judged." Gabriel Marcel called this the key to an authentic metaphysics of man. We must never judge others without realising that we are ourselves judged by what we are saying in condemnation of others. Moral condemnation must always in the first instance be directed at our own selves. We must judge as we would ourselves wish to be judged. We must judge in willingness to forgive; as we, even when we speak, recognise our own need to be forgiven.

To say all this is not to detract one whit from the right and the duty to condemn evil. It constitutes no condoning of evil, it amounts to no "soft words" about evil. Sometimes it is rather lightly said: "To understand all is to forgive all." But "to understand all", is to understand one's own need to be forgiven, hence one's need to *deserve* forgiveness. This rules out what we might call "forgiveness on the cheap". There is no forgiveness without recognition of guilt-that-needs-forgiveness. Hence the words "I forgive you" are not lightly spoken to others, because they cannot lightly be accepted by oneself. In a true sense the most cruel thing we can say to another, the greatest insult we can inflict on the human dignity of

another, is to say that you forgive him because he was not
responsible for what he was doing. This is in fact to regard
him as lacking power to choose, lacking freedom, lacking a
sense of right and wrong, and therefore as being less than
human. But on the other hand, it is equally and very similarly
insulting to a man to say that his evil deeds are such that he is
obviously outside the moral society of the speaker. This is
precisely what moralistic denunciation often seems to do.

Moralistic denunciation is directed at the evildoer in
person and tends to abound in language stressing his total
exclusion from the society of the speaker. It emphasises
the radical separation and distinction of the speaker from
the sinner. It can come close to thanking God that one is not
a sinner like X. Moralistic denunciation is made readily, gladly,
sometimes jubilantly, nearly always self-righteously. It can
give real emotional satisfaction to the speaker, stemming
from and manifesting a sense of hiw own obvious moral
superiority. Because it carries no component of awareness
of being oneself under judgement, it does not have to convey
compassion or mercy; or to suggest belief in the possibility
of repentance; or to carry with it a promise of forgiveness.
It judges without any sense of one's self as needing forgiveness. It does not offer compassion or mercy because there is
not admission that one needs compassion and mercy oneself.

Moralistic denunciation comes sometimes from people who
seem to be welcoming the chance to say: "I told you so.
These people were never capable of anything else but crime –
and now you have proof of it."

There is too much moralistic denunciation in our society;
and too little attempt to understand, too little recognition of
the sins and omissions of our society and all its members in
creating or tolerating conditions in which evil flourishes.

In respect of denunciation of deeds of violence there is
a special need to beware not to become oneself infected by
the spirit of the very violence which one is condemning. We
tend to become infected by the evil we are combatting. We
tend to *become* the thing we hate. Hate is a contagious disease. By hating violent men, we can ourselves become violent
men, consumed by a desire to crush, to destroy, to eliminate.
This merely spreads violence further. Violence can be killed
only by love, love expressed in the readiness to forgive, love

expressed in the structures of a loving and therefore reconciled and just society. Forgiveness can come only through sharing in the power of Christ's prayer on the Cross: "Father, forgive them. They do not know what they are doing."

The lessons of violence

These observations, I believe, are relevant to any judgements passed from "outside" on the people in the North who have been the victims of campaigns of violence over the past ten years. We must resist the tendency to say that such violence is "typical of the bigoted people of the North". We must resist any temptation to feel, "so long as it stays up there, and does not come down here, it will not be so bad!"

For too long too many in the Republic seemed concerned mainly to keep the violence "up there". This was always an illusion and can now be seen to be an impossibility. Violent crime is becoming a standard part of our experience in the Republic. Armed robbery is now an everyday occurrence across the country. There is no way of knowing at first glance how much of this is "political", how much is "ordinary" crime; but this is in itself significant. Both of these phenomena alike are the direct consequence of the Northern campaign of violence. We are being dragged by our professed "liberators" into a situation of endemic violent crime such as used to be associated with people like the Mafia or with the Chicago of Al Capone. To that extent the campaign is being waged against Ireland and not for Ireland. Are the leaders utterly and incurably blind to what they are doing to the country they profess to love?

One aspect of the years of violence in the North which we in the South should ponder carefully is that the Northern violence absorbs into itself much of the endemic violence which affects underprivileged sectors of large modern cities everywhere. This violence (we are sadly inclined nowadays to call it "ordinary urban violence"), which elsewhere shows itself as vandalism, mugging, etc., is something which seems alas to face all modern societies. I fear that our complacency about Northern violence, our tendency to say that it is due to some peculiar wickedness of the people "up there", could be rudely upset if or when we came ourselves to be afflicted with violence on a larger scale in our society. We are not sensitive enough to the existence in our society of the sort of conditions which breed violence.

Violence, I believe, results sometimes from the frustration of people who would never otherwise be listened to or have their grievances recognised. When one comes to think of it, is it not the case that there are sectors of the population, expecially in our towns and cities, of which we do not seem to become aware until some of their inhabitants engage in vandalism or violence? It is almost as though they felt they had to engage in destruction before we could be brought to realise that they were there at all.

One has only to walk through some of the ghetto neighbourhoods in Northern cities to realise that the social and housing conditions there were breeding grounds for urban violence long before the present campaign erupted. Row after row of identical "concrete box" houses, with no human dimension to them, no community centre, no children's playgrounds, no youth recreational or social amenties. The Irish Bishops, in their joint Pastoral Letter, *Human Life is Sacred,* in 1977, spoke of such housing developments as "social time-bombs with slow-burning fuses". Our own society here does not always seem to have got the message.

It will understandably be argued that it is difficult to find the money for such facilities as leisure amenities for children and youth. What is certain, however, is that it will cost the nation much more, in the not distant future, in terms of malicious injury claims, rehabilitation of young offenders, the prison service etc., to cope with the vandalism and violence when they happen, than it would cost to provide the preventive services now.

Many social investigations have been done of the Northern violence. It has been correlated with religious denomination, educational achievement, etc.. A correlation which needs seriously to be studied is its correlation with unemployment and other forms of deprivation. The chronic unemployment, extending back for generations now in West Belfast and in Derry and in other Northern cities with "nationalist" majorities, certainly had, and continues to have, an important causative role in violence. I wonder if, as a nation, we are sufficiently aware of the grave risks we in this society of ours are running with unemployment, expecially of youth. I wonder do we expect the Government, or some other "them", to make unemployment go away, without any special effort or restraint on our part? Or are we conscious that what we do and fail to do ourselves, individually and as co-responsible members of our professional organisations, trade unions, etc., is decisive for the overcoming of this grave national disorder?

Northern violence is clearly correlated also with the sense of perpetual exclusion of one sector of the population from access to power and opportunity and from sharing in decision-making. Until that situation is changed by radically new political and social structures, there can be little hope that violence will cease. Violence is being fostered now by the sense of an absence of an official policy which would guarantee that such really new political and social structures were going to be created. Cosmetic exercises in redescribing inequalities and injustices are not going to convince the excluded that there will be a fair place and a new deal for them in Northern society. We here need to have social antennae sensitised to pick up the sounds of grievance or protest from socially deprived or excluded sectors of our own society.

But let me make perfectly plain my conviction that one of the tragedies of violence is that, far from remedying injustice, it is merely creating new injustices. I do not hesitate to say that it has caused more deprivation, hardship and intractable demoralisation among the minority community than did even the situation from which it professes to be liberating them. Violence has called attention to voices too long ignored by State establishments. But the strings it now sounds are false. Violence, so far from eradicating injustice, is now merely introducing new factors of injustice into the situation. So far from liberating the oppressed, it is blinding them into new and worse forms of oppression, of which violence, murder and hate are themselves the chief. One of the most urgent demands of justice in the North, and specifically of justice for the minority, at this time, is that those responsible for continuing a campaign of revolutionary violence should desist.

Our unarmed police

We Irish, I submit, are not a violent people, whether North

or South, whether Protestant or Catholic. Once conditions of sharing and partnership and therefore hope of justice are established, the basic non-violence of the Irish people shows itself.

Our experience in the Republic is reassuring in this regard. One of the bravest and most enlightened decisions of the founders of this State was the decision to have an unarmed police force – and this while civil war violence was still raging. This decision was, I suggest, almost unprecedented in the history of post-revolution societies. Due tribute has rarely been paid to it. It is a pity that it was not then imitated in the North. It was an act of faith in the basic non-violence of the Irish people. It was an act of confidence which was amply rewarded and vindicated. We were one of the few Western societies which from the thirties through the fifties was able to close down and abandon prisons, turning this one into a site for a university extension, that one into the site for a Cathedral. The unarmed and essentially non-violent nature and tradition of our police service contributed significantly to that situation.

The Garda Síochána – we did not even call them police, because of the earlier association of that name with violence – became, I believe, one of the best police forces in the world. I am convinced that it can still give a lead to the world in the study and practice of non-violent methods and techniques of coping with political subversion, with violent crime, with crowd- or "demo"-control and with law-enforcement among the young. Most societies nowadays expend huge sums in learning techniques of violence, to be used, of course, in combatting violence. But there is a paradox in using violence to eradicate violence. There could even, in some circumstances, be a self-contradiction.

There is surely evidence from other societies, and specifically from the North in recent years, that certain forms of counter-violence can create a "spirit of violence", which generates new violence in a vicious ongoing causal circle. Such methods can "recycle" violence rather than eliminate it. I believe that if even a fraction of the money spent by modern societies on violent counter-violence were devoted to research into techniques of non-violence, we could thereby reap more fruits of peace. To set a headline by promoting just this kind of research would, I believe, be fully in line with the noble history, the tradition and the spirit of our Garda Síochána. The preservation of the unarmed character and non-violent tradition of the Gardaí is more than ever desirable today. With the Gardaí exposed to violence and even armed attack, it is also going to be more than ever difficult. It is fully understandable that they should demand protection and safeguards. Ultimately this protection and these safeguards can come only from the unqualified support of public opinion and the cooperation of the public with the Gardaí in their difficult and even dangerous service to the safety and security of us all. Any campaign of denigration of the Garda Síochána is anti-social, unpatriotic and reprehensible.

This is also a time when no slightest handle or pretext must be given to any such campaign of denigration. Our Gardaí have the noble task of earning respect for the law by their example, as well as and even before enforcing it by their lawful power. They have the patrotic mission of respecting human rights and the dignity of the person as well as protecting those rights and that dignity against malefactors. The Garda Síochána has carried out that task and discharged that mission honourably. They have learned the lesson written in all the pages of history, and more especially of Irish history, and evident in contemporary experience across the globe, that counter-violence never eliminates violence, it only feeds it.

The true antidote to violence, whether political or criminal, at this time can only be non-violent policing techniques, exercised in absolute respect for human dignity, even that of those who deny the rights and dignity of others. The police of a newly independent Ireland gave an historic lead in replacing military-style law-enforcement in Ireland by a truly "Civic Guard" force, who were, in a genuine sense, citizens guarding the peace of the citizens for the citizens of this country. I believe the Irish police can still give unique witness to the world of peace-keeping without arms, without violence, with respect for the personal dignity of offenders. It is not sentiment but realism to affirm that law and law-custodians should be respected rather than feared.

Capital punishment
It is sometimes believed that, in the contemporary situation,

peace-keeping requires the restoration or retention of ultimate deterrents like the death penalty. There are undoubtedly aspects of this question which can be properly addressed only by those responsible for security. It is with utmost deference to their responsible and informed opinion that one ventures to speak of it. Yet I feel bound to say that, from the moral point of view, it seems to me that the case *for* capital punishment is by no means conclusive. I at once add that I do not think the moral case against capital punishment is absolutely incontestable either. Yet I am convinced that there has been growing moral insight into the question of punishment and sanctions in general and into capital punishment in particular; and that this growing insight makes the traditional case for capital punishment less and less convincing. As to its supposed deterrent value, this is something which is amenable to testing by empirical evidence. A volume of evidence exists, suggesting that capital punishment is not necessary and perhaps not even effective as a deterrent. In the circumstances of Ireland at this time, I believe that recourse to the death penalty would simply feed the terrorism which it might be invoked to quell and would contribute further to the depreciation of the sense of the sacredness of human life, which is our greatest national tragedy at this time.

Both psychology and honest moral self-discernment reveal murky depths of what we can only call latent sadism in our instinctual reaction to public enemies or public criminals. We have to bring the Gospel right down into those murky depths, redeeming the passions so that they may not lead us to *become* that thing which we hate and fear. All of us in this country have a personal responsibility to ensure that we do not become emotionally or morally poisoned by the violence we abhor; that we do not ourselves become violent and vengeful in our determination to crush violence and crime in society. I suggest that we can find in the North plenty of evidence to deter us from any temptation to security excesses. One contributing factor in the continuation of the Provisional I.R.A. campaign has incontestably been the repeated blunders and excesses of the security forces and their consequent complete failure to win credibility or confidence in the Catholic areas most affected by the violence.

Instruments of peace

This chapter began with a form of prayerful mediation on the beatitudes. It has in part taken the form of a moral sermon. It has also dealt with matters which are clearly matters of politics. I make no apology for this mingling of genres. Prayer must lead into life, must issue in action. We have the words of the Lord himself to affirm it: "Not everyone who says to me, Lord, Lord, will enter the Kingdom of heaven; but he who does the will of my Father, who is in heaven" (*Matthew* 7:21). Sermons must aim to motivate for action. Sermons are, all of them, in one way or another, appeals to repentance, to conversion; and conversion, or *metanoia,* is a radical change, in the spirit of the Gospel, of our patterns of behaviour. It was Karl Barth, and no contemporary "liberation theologian", who said that every Christian sermon must, in the last analysis, be also political.

I shall, therefore, end with a prayer, as I began with a meditation. It is the immortal prayer left us by one who outstandingly lived in the spirit of the beatitudes, the Poverello of Assisi, St Francis. Let the prayer of St Francis be not only our prayer; let it also be the reality of our lives and the pattern of our behaviour.

> Lord, make me an instrument of thy peace.
> Where there is hatred, let me sow love;
> where there is injury, pardon;
> where there is doubt, faith;
> where there is despair, hope;
> where there is sadness, joy;
> where there is darkness, light.
>
> O Divine Master, grant that I may not
> so much seek to be consoled, as to console;
> not so much to be understood, as to understand;
> not so much to be loved, as to love;
> For it is in giving that we receive,
> it is in pardoning that we are pardoned,
> it is in dying that we are born again to eternal life.

THOU SHALT NOT KILL

Beginning with the year 1968, and for each of the eleven years up to 1978, the last year of his life, Pope Paul, on each successive New Year's day, addressed urgent pleas to the peoples of the earth to think, pray, plan and work for peace. Yet it is not peace which seems to prevail, but war, military coup, kidnap and hijack, violence and the counter-violence of reprisal, repression and torture, all of them manifestations of the cult of violence and of brute force. There would seem plenty of reasons why the Pope might have felt discouraged. This made only the more impressive the calm and patient and unwearying perseverance of his efforts for peace. His persistence resembled St Paul's own, expressed in such words as:

> Never give in, my dear brothers, never admit defeat; keep on working at the Lord's work always, knowing that, in the Lord, you cannot be labouring in vain (1 *Corinthians* 15 : 58).

In Ireland, the prayers and longings for peace of nearly the whole population, the appeals for peace of so many political and community leaders, might well be counted a dismal failure as we look back sadly on ten years of explosion, assassination, intimidation and extortion. But in Ireland, as in the world, this is no time to be discouraged or to desist. It would be tragic if violence were to continue to pile up corpses, ruins and tears for more years to come. But it could be more tragic still if violence were to seem to succeed and if evil means were supposed to be made right because they got results. The final triumph of evil would be if good men came to feel that perhaps after all evil succeeds and therefore cannot be totally wrong; or at least that it is useless to go on resisting it because up to now it has proved irresistible.

One of the truths most strongly asserted in the Bible is

that evil is strong with a strength which is more than natural, indeed a strength which is supernatural. Evil is pervasive and persuasive, deceptive, resourceful, subtle. Evil has been a powerful presence throughout all human history. Sin has a mighty grip on human affairs. St Paul declares:

> It is not against human enemies that we have to struggle, but against the Sovereignties and the Powers who originate the darkness in this world, the spiritual army of evil in the heavens. That is why you must rely on God's armour, or you will not be able to put up any resistance when the worst happens, or have enough resources to hold your ground (*Ephesians* 6:12-13).

The Bible teaches that evil is powerful; but that it will not prevail against the mightier power of Christ. But it is only in Christ that we can have the power to conquer evil. The armour of our struggle against the evil of violence is our faith in Christ: "this is the victory which overcomes the world, our faith" (1 *John* 5 : 4).

The struggle against violence and for peace in Ireland is a struggle for the survival of values which are not only insepar- able from Christian faith and basic Christian morality but are also the condition for all civilised living, those values, namely, which are expressed in the principle, human life is sacred. The future of Christianity in Ireland, the future of all human rights and freedoms in Ireland, are imperilled if the funda- mental principle of the sacredness of human life is weakened. It cannot be denied that, after ten years of murder and violent death, that principle has been gravely weakened.

It has been obviously weakened in the minds of those who planned and ordered the horrible deaths of these years. It has been weakened in the hearts of those who, under orders, have had to perpetrate these deeds. These are frequently very young. Killing does not come naturally to them. They were not born killers. They have to be trained to do it. Other and older men have made killers of them; sometimes making them what Pope Paul called "blind and fanatic killers of their brethren who in themselves are innocent". Heavy indeed is the responsibility of those who channel the intelligence and idealism of youth into the bestial business of killing.

But even among the population as a whole, who reject and abhor violence, the sense of the sacredness of human life, of the awfulness of assassination, blood-feud and bomb-carnage, becomes gradually blunted. We adjust ourselves to these evils and in the process they come to seem less evil. News that a few years ago would have filled us for days with horror and revulsion may now evoke only a shrug and its traces will be obliterated within hours by the unending chatter of later newscasts. "Human kind," said T. S. Eliot, "cannot bear very much reality." We cannot bear much of the reality of evil. But what we often do is to make the evil bearable and acceptable by renaming it "normal" or "inevitable" or "perfectly understandable in the circumstances". Have we not to confess, to our shame, that sometimes the killings have seemed rather more "understandable" if done by "one of ours", and more awful and more "typical" if done by "one of them".

It has become difficult to keep count even of the dead, much more of the maimed and the bereaved, the nerve-shattered, those made homeless, jobless or driven to emigrate by the violence. In any case, statistics also have diminishing impact; turning people into statistics can be another way of softening the blow of reality. But as well as people, something else is being slowly killed amongst us – and that is our horror at killing, our perception of the utter foulness and evil of it. Some years ago, outrage was evoked by the phrase, "acceptable level of violence". Now this is in practice what almost all are prepared to settle for. We can almost forget that "acceptable level of violence" means "acceptable number of murders every week". Can there be, in a Christian or even in just a civilised society, an "acceptable number" of killings?

The evil of murder

It may indeed be difficult or even impossible to eliminate killing altogether from society. Some of the methods proposed for doing so (like ruthless repression, savage security measures, the return of the death penalty) might only serve to add new sources and new forms of violence to those it is proposed to eliminate. It is the word "acceptable" which is worrying. To find killings "acceptable" might mean to find their evil acceptable; and this would be to begin to be contaminated by that evil, to begin to be oneself made evil by it.

Why then is killing of the innocent so unacceptably evil? If we do not see its evil, then we are indeed in need of radical conversion — conversion to humanity as well as conversion to Christianity. Awareness that God is God and awareness that man is man are both involved in the sense of the sacredness of human life. When this sense is damaged, all the resources of faith and of grace as well as of reason and love and the experience of being loved are needed for its repair. The reflections one advances in support of the proposition that human life is sacred, that deliberate killing of the innocent is evil, are not given as "proofs": in a real sense, one *sees* the truth of these propositions rather than waits for them to be proven before assenting to them. But reflections drawn from faith and from human experience can correct the impairment of sight which prevents our clear vision of reality.

The truth revealed to us by God about the creation of man is that man is made in the image of God. The truth revealed by God about the new creation of man in Christ is that man is remade as the son of God by being made brother of Christ and son of the Father in the only-begotten Son of the Father who is Christ. These truths are repeated so often that our attention is no longer pricked by their sound; we mentally "switch off" or "lower the sound" when we hear them. We need an effort to realise them, to make them *real* for ourselves.

"The image of God" is found in man; therefore man is that part of creation which most resembles God. To know man truly and fully would also be to know something about God. If we are to know God at all it must be chiefly from the recognition of man that we will derive our knowledge of him. To kill a man is to kill, in so far as it is in our power to do so, something of God. It is to kill in ourselves some of our own capacity for knowing God. In a real sense, to kill a man is to reveal that we do not know God at all and that we lie to ourselves and to others when we say we know him or love him St John says this even about hating a man, and hating can be an implicit wish to kill or to see someone killed. St John says:

> Anyone who says, "I love God",
> and hates his brother
> is a liar,
> since a man who does not love the brother that he can see
> cannot love God, whom he has never seen (1 *John* 4 : 20).

Believing in God is not a matter of words: unless words come alive in deeds they are only noise. To believe in God means also to know that he loves all men, that he is lovable; it means to love him and to love men as he loves them. St John introduces the above words by saying:

> God is love
> and anyone who lives in love lives in God
> and God lives in him (1 *John* 4 : 16).

Whatever "Cause" it be that we have made our god-substitute, it is not the Living God we are believing in if we plan or do death to the innocent.

God is life; to believe in him is to believe in the God of the living. To plan or to do death to others is equivalently to deny the living God, or to say absurdly "God is dead", or to wish insanely that God were dead. St John implies this when he says:

> We have passed out of death and into life
> and of this we can be sure
> because we love our brothers.
> If you refuse to love, you must remain dead;
> to hate your brother is to be a murderer,
> and murderers, as you know, do not
> have eternal life in them (1 *John* 3 : 15).

Man is made for God

The reason why man is the summit of creation is that man alone in creation can know and love God. Creation comes into its own through man. Why? Because creation comes into its own when it comes back to God in whom it began. This can happen only when man stands upright on the surface of Planet Earth, raises hands and eyes to heaven and says: "God be praised." The greatest thing that man can ever do is to pray. Man was made for prayer. Creation was made for prayer; its whole purpose was that on a tiny planet amid the immeasurable distances of the universe, after the uncounted millions of years of evolution, there might be at last a creature capable of prayer. To end a life is to leave a man no more time to pray, no time to make his soul, no time to repent, no time to begin again, or perhaps to begin at all, his real life's work, which is to know and love God. To kill is to rob God of the praise and love and service he was due from a man he made only for this; and that special praise and love and service can never come from any other.

We can argue, and it is true, that man is unique because he alone among living things has reason. But the supreme act of this reason is to acknowledge God; and until God is acknowledged man has not fully attained "the use of reason" or really "come of age". We can argue, and it is true, that man is unique because he alone among creatures is free. But the fullest exercise of freedom is to choose for God, to choose to believe in him and to accept his love. Until God is known as love, man has not wholly known what love means. Unless God is loved, a man may die without ever fully having loved. To kill is not merely to extinguish a source of love and an object of love at the human level; it is to deprive a man of his time for loving God and to rob God of the love that was his due from this living man.

At the philosophical level, murder must be pronounced intrinsically and absolutely immoral. The human person is an absolute moral value and must be treated always as an end, never merely as a means; always as a person, never as a thing. This is because man is both subject and object of moral values. What affects man in his existence, dignity and rights, affects the very essence of morality. Sartre was only expressing in different language a classical principle of the natural law moral tradition when he said: "Man is the bearer of moral value. Man is the being through whom value comes into the world."

Such also is the ethical implication of the Christ-centred humanism of Pope John II, as so powerfully expressed in his first encyclical, *Redemptor Hominis*. Here we read:

> Man in the full truth of his existence, of his personal being and also of his community and social being — in the sphere of his own family in the sphere of society and very diverse contexts, in the sphere of his own nation or people (perhaps still only that of his clan or tribe), and in the sphere of the whole of mankind — this man is the primary route that the Church must travel in fulfilling her mission: he is the primary and fundamental way for the Church, the way traced out by Christ himself, the way that leads invariably through the mystery of the Incarnation and the Redemption.

The absolute and grave wrongness of murder derives from this fact. To kill a man is absolutely immoral, because it is to annihilate a source of morals. It can never be moral to extinguish a source of morals.

Hatred and all forms of discrimination, exploitation, racialism, are immoral for the same reason. They are forms of symbolic murder. They annihilate the Other as person, as moral subject, as liberty, in order to relegate him to the non-human, non-moral world of things. The language here is existentialist; but the teaching is the same as Christ's. Christ taught that to hate is forbidden by the same commandment which prohibits murder; because hatred is at its limit a wish that the other did not exist. The language and behaviour of hatred itself shows this: it speaks of "cutting a person dead".

At the human level, there is an irrational self-contradiction involved in killing the innocent in the name of freedom; for we extinguish a freedom when we end a life. But there is a still more blasphemous self-contradiction involved when it is Christians who kill; for we deny the living and loving Father of Our Lord Jesus Christ when we kill.

At the level of political philosophy, there is an inherent self-contradiction involved in seeking to kill, or even intimidate, coerce or crush dissenters. Democracy is dialogue. It is negated when we impose the silence of the grave on those who disagree; or when we drive our of our society or community or street those "of the other kind". Democracy is reasonable discussion, persuasion, conviction. It dies when we replace persuasion by force and treat others as objects to be bombed into unwilling submission, not persons to be persuaded into free consent. We cannot build a free and democratic society on the denial to fellow-citizens of the most basic of all human rights, the right to live.

Brothers of Christ

When we include Christ in our thinking about man and society, still more dimensions of the evil of killing become apparent. Christ so loves man as to dwell among them, "pitch his tent" in the midst of them, throw in his lot with them in their march through history. These are among the various levels of meaning implied by St John's words in the Prologue to his Gospel: "The Word was made flesh and dwelt amongst us". To men he gave "power to become sons of God". It is this God-given power which is impiously disposed of by man when a killer presses a trigger or plants a bomb. Man is the glory of creation. But this is because he reflects the glory of God, because he has the capacity to live for God's glory. St Irenaeus said: "The glory of God is living man." The full meaning of these words is: "The glory of God is the living man who is Christ, and every man who is living with Christ's life." The ultimate evil of murder is revealed by Christ. It is to negate and do to death, in so far as this lies in our power, the Christ-life and the Christ-love which are present in a living man. It is Christ a man hates, tortures, crucifies and kills when he does to death those whom Christ calls brothers, those in whom Christ personally lives. It is the cries of the Good Friday mob that are re-echoed when people say about "the other sort", "away with them", or when we argue: "Yes, killing is terrible, but it does get results"; or when we say: "I condemn violence; but in the circumstances it is perfectly understandable". It is now, while there is still time to change, that we must try to take the full impact into our thoughts and feelings and attitudes and judgements of the final and de-cisive words of Christ in judgement: "In so far as you did this to one of the least of these brothers of mine, you did it to me" (*Matthew* 25 : 40).

Nationalism: true and false

If I am asked whether Christianity has not failed in this Irish crisis, I can only answer that Christianity has not failed, but we Christians have failed Christianity. Christ has not failed; the Church has not failed. But many of us have not found room for Christ in our emotions and personal and social relations: we treated him as an outsider to our politics, to our reading of our revolutionary history, to our view of nationalism. In many areas of our personal and civic lives we treated him as a stranger and never made him welcome (cf. *Matthew* 25 : 43). Some people have not listened to Christ speaking to us in his Church or to the Church speaking to us about Christ. Too many times we have hardened our per-sonal and nationalistic hearts and made false Gods and false

Christs for ourselves out of nationalisms and false patriotisms.

The way of return to Christ's true message of peace and love will be long. It demands what Pope Paul called "a work of continual therapy". In Ireland today it demands a reappraisal and renewal of our concept of nationalism. Sometimes this has merited the warnings of Pope Paul about a nationalism "which exaggerates national expression to the point of collective egoism and exclusivist antagonism". Many are already rejecting this martial type of nationalism sometimes found in our tradition; but some of them seem to go on to decry and to try to weaken any sense of national distinctiveness, any pride in our past or aspiration to cultural and national identity. This reaction is exaggerated, intolerant and harmful. Authentic nationalism is legitimate and can even be virtuous; nations, each in their fashion, contribute to the many-sided richness of the inheritance of humanity. We owe it to the rest of the world as well as to ourselves to remain ourselves in an age of growing alienation, rootlessness and historical and cultural amnesia. What we need more and more for the future is formation in positive, mature and open nationalism, with emphasis on being "with others" in one Europe and one world, rather than on "ourselves alone" against others. We need a nationalism deeply penetrated by Christian faith, a nationalism with its emphasis on cultural and spiritual and religious values and not one-sidedly on revolutions and battles and fighting men; a nationalism which exalts the arts of peace above the deeds of war; a nationalism which demonstrates that the non-violent politics of peace is a better way to justice than is violence.

Obedience does not excuse

Such being the human and the Christian vision of life, such being the basis of its dignity and sacredness and inviolability in human and in Christian reality, the question must be asked, how it has come about that some people have been able so to forget this vision tht they can coldly and callously kill, without apparent trouble of conscience. Many of these were brought up in a Christian tradition, or had a Christian background. Those with whom I, as Catholic Bishop, am primarily concerned are those who were brought up in a Catholic tradition or had a Catholic background.

Undoubtedly, as I have argued in an earlier chapter, much of this perversion of conscience has come about through a process of thorough indoctrination in the ideology of "the Cause"; this "Cause" being, in effect, regarded as an absolute, virtually "beyond good and evil"; in other words, being turned into a god-substitute, and being accorded the absolute rights and authority, and treated as deserving the unquestioning obedience, which belongs to the true God alone. Such is the nature of an ideology; and, for militant republicans, republicanism has become an ideology, a veritable substitute religion. I have already argued that it is, in fact, a secularised form of Christianity.

Recruits are initiated into this movement and indoctrinated with this ideology from a very young age. The involvement with violence may, in fact, begin already in primary schooldays. One of the ugliest aspects of republican violence is that it has, since the beginning, used school-children as "riot-fodder". There is evidence, in fact, that parents may be intimidated into allowing their children to partake in the stone-throwing and other violent activities which are a standard part of the ritual Provo protest-happenings. The indoctrination becomes more intense at secondary-school level, when young people can be enticed into the Fianna or other republican youth organisations, and carefully schooled in the ideology and ethics of violence, and later into the use of its weapons of death. One of the horrifying pictures of recent times was that of a teenage girl brandishing a large revolver: innocence in the warm glow of springtide life, already frozen into the cold, rigid hardness of the killer.

A further factor in the turning of youths into killers has been the imbedding into them, throughout their training, of the notion of blind and absolute obedience to "higher orders". This obedience is reinforced by the administering of an oath, marking formal admission into "the Movement". An atmosphere of drama, indeed of quasi-religious solemnity, surrounds the taking of the oath — an atmosphere calculated to have profound emotional impact on impressionable youths. From this point on "the Movement", "the Cause", take on something of the absoluteness which belongs properly to God; and "superior orders" become a kind of substitute conscience. All this, together with the totally ruthless penalties enforced against "deserters" or suspected informers, is enough to ensure that orders, however heartless, are carried out.

The first comment one must make on this is that this century, more than most, has manifested the incalculable evil introduced into human history in the name of "obedience to higher authority". This was, in fact, precisely the plea entered in exculpation of their heinous behaviour by many of the Nazi accused during and since the Nuremberg hearings.

A recent study by a City University of New York psychologist sheds further light upon this problem, and I find his study of remarkable relevance to the methods practised by paramilitary groups in Ireland. I refer to the book, *Obedience to Authority,* by Stanley Milgram (1974).

Milgram conducted a series of experiments which indicated, in a frightening fashion, how, in the name of obedience (in the case in question in his book, to the director of the "experiments"), ordinary, decent, humane and kindly people are prepared to perform tasks involving the infliction of extreme pain, even to the point of lethal pain, upon others — tasks which they would never, in any circumstances, have contemplated were it not for their passive submission to "authority".

In his own enlightening reflections on his experimental discoveries Milgram remarks:

> The force exerted by the moral sense of the individual is less effective than social myth would have us believe. Though such prescriptions as "Thou shalt not kill" occupy a pre-eminent place in the moral order, they do not occupy a correspondingly intractable position in human psychic structure.

One of the mechanisms which, he concludes, enable "moral factors to be shunted aside with relative ease" is "the tendency of the individual to become so absorbed in the narrow technical aspect of the task that he loses sight of its broader consequences". It is interesting here to note the stress which the Provisional I.R.A. place upon their constantly "improved technology". Presumably many of their bomb-making experts are able to concentrate on the technical aspects of their task to a point when they become oblivious of the picture of the pieces of human beings which will later, because of their "technology", be picked up and placed in pathetic plastic bags or in sad, premature coffins.

Common to all the examples studied by Milgram is, he concludes, "the disappearance of a sense of responsibility". This disappearance is most commonly brought about by appeal to some abstract principle, such as a "noble cause"; or by getting the subjects to "see their behaviour in a larger context that is benevolent and useful to society — the pursuit of scientific truth".

In the conditioning of people to kill, torture and destroy, a crucial factor is "the intense devaluation of the victim prior to action against him".

Milgram finds that many of the subjects were able to content themselves with interior and silent dissent from the prescribed behaviour. Their strictly private moral disapproval of their actions was somehow felt to detach the agent from his action and to make his action a responsibility of others rather than of himself. In a curious way, this seemed to make immoral behaviour more likely rather than less likely to be performed. Milgram comments:

> Tyrannies are perpetuated by diffident men who do not possess the courage to act out their beliefs. Time and again in the experiment people disvalued what they were doing but could not muster the inner resources to translate their values into action . . . The person who assumes full responsibility for the act has evaporated. Perhaps this is the most common characteristic of socially organised evil in modern society.

Responsibility for acts of violence

Some of Milgram's comments have an appalling actuality in Ireland today. His analysis of how men and boys can be conditioned into perpetrating callous murder and horrible crime with apparent ease of conscience is all too accurate in the daily record of "the people we are" — or at least some of us are — in this island now. The blunting of consciences — older theologians spoke of the "callousing" of consciences — takes many of the forms detected in Milgram's experiments. "Commanders' orders" have been throughout history, up to and including Auschwitz, the Ardeatine Caves and My Lai, the commonest substitute and alibi for personal conscience.

In modern revolutionary movements, "commanders' orders" tend to be much more ruthless and the penalties for disobedience more savage, than in regular armies.

"The intense devaluation of the victim prior to action against him" is a marked feature of both varieties of paramilitary bodies in action in this country. Those who kill scarcely see themselves as killing human beings; they are only "hitting legitimate targets", "executing selected enemy personnel" (like, for example, seventy-nine-year-old Lord Mountbatten on a family fishing holiday), "liquidating agents of British capitalist interests", "paying back the Brits", "deterring sectarian killers" (by, of all things, a matching set of sectarian killings); or else, on the loyalist paramilitary side, they are "exterminating terrorists", "restoring law and order", "teaching disloyalists a needed lesson", "hitting back at the Republic". The Vietnam atrocities were possible because G.I.'s were schooled to think of the Vietcong as "gooks", therefore less than human; even the term "V.C.'s" already dehumanised them into some sort of dangerous foliage. The term, "the Brits", serves a similar role for one main group of combatants in Ireland now, as does "Fenians" for the other.

The dissociation of agent from action can also be seen at work. The killers and bombers do not wait to see the victim, the blood, the agony; to hear the moans of pain, to watch the tears of loved ones. It is just one more "military mission successfully accomplished". Those who direct over-all strategy are, of course, usually remote from bullets and bombs and therefore detached from awareness of the bleeding and weeping consequences of "military orders".

Over-arching everything, of course, is the phenomenon of "the Cause", that great and quasi-divine abstraction which makes killing sacred and evil good. It is something worth reflecting on that, in this country, the term "political crime" is sometimes emotionally felt as though it were the name of a virtue.

We churchmen have exhausted the language of moral condemnation in respect of deeds of violence. We have made repeated appeals to the consciences of those engaged in them, as well as of the public at large. Sad experience has shown, of course, the limitations of moral exhortation and of appeal to conscience. One must stress also the political structural changes which are necessary to establish the justice, mutual inter-community trust and partnership without which there cannot be peace. Nevertheless, the appeal to conscience is paramount, and I believe that our appeals have not been fruitless and that there is now, both North and South of the Border, a whole people's revulsion from violence, awareness of its moral evil and rejection of its mythology, such as have scarcely been seen here for fifty years.

Nor must one despair of a change of heart, an awakening of conscience, on the part of the leadership and the rank and file of the paramilitary groups themselves. I will speak directly here only of the republican leadership and combatants. Presumably, "Protestant" terrorists will not know or heed what might be said by a Catholic Bishop. The I.R.A. leaders or members may shout back: "What about the others? What about the sectarian killings? What about the brutalities of the Brits? What about Girdwood and Hollywood and Bloody Sunday and H-Block . . .?" I would appeal to them to remember that "whataboutery" is one of the commonest forms of evasion of personal moral responsibility. It is one of the routine retorts of those who try, in Milgram's words, to shunt aside moral factors which might deter one from persisting in one's course of action. To have a conscience is to say, not, "What about X and Y . . .?"; but, "What about *me*?" The dissociation of the person from his acts and the related dissociation of "the Cause" or "the Movement" from acts done in its name are, to quote Milgram again, the "most common characteristic of socially organised evil in modern society".

Dishonouring the republican tradition

"The Cause" in fact must be morally judged by the sum of the actions done in its name. In the case in question, the historic republican cause is being systematically morally contaminated by the deeds now been perpetrated by order of those leaders now claiming to represent it. This is having far-reaching consequences for the whole Irish national consciousness, consequences which those leaders must surely themselves deplore. They sometimes voice indignation at the decline in patriotism, the loss of the sense of national identity, the lack of pride in our past and confidence in our future, which they rightly see in Ireland today. What they refuse to admit is that these very phenomena have for one of their chief causes the very campaign of physical force which they are themselves waging. But this is the reality. This is one of the main sources of our national sickness at this time. Indeed we could well borrow the words of Tone, hallowed in national tradition, and say that the republican campaign of today is itself the "never-failing source of (most of) our political evils". It certainly is making well-nigh unimaginable for generations to come the dream of Tone, "to unite the whole of Ireland and to abolish the memory of all past dissensions".

The present campaign is not only murdering and causing murder of those whom historic republicanism aspired to unite. It is not only bombing and destroying our cities and towns and our factories: and incidentally it is surely unusual in the annals of guerilla movements when destruction of their own cities and buildings is claimed as victories and as military successes. The campaign is not only crippling our hopes and efforts at national economic survival and thus bombing our future. The campaign is also bombing our past. The name and the honour of the dead generations are being discredited; the whole of their noble achievement is being put at risk.

It is within the capacity of a small number of men to bring this disastrous campaign to an end. Few of these men or their "volunteers" are what would ordinarily be called psychopaths or "criminal types". Undoubtedly, a movement which makes fanatical dedication its mystique and killing its immediate objective will attract its quota of criminal or psychopathic personalities. Some, however, of those who became involved in these movements had, at least to start with, a certain idealism, a certain nobility. They can show courage, endurance, a spirit of sacrifice – although it must be remembered that qualities such as these are no guarantee of honour or virtue in a movement; they were found in plenty among Hitler's Gauleiters and Stalin's Commissars.

I would wish, however, to appeal to the better instincts and the calmer consciences of those involved in the militant republican movement. I cannot doubt but that conscience sometimes disturbs them. I would say to them that they are better men and better Irishmen in those moments when that conscience is subject to disquiet and to doubt than when it is serene and untroubled. To seek urgent ways of ending their campaign would be neither cowardly nor dishonourable. It would be the bravest, noblest and most honourable thing they ever did for Ireland. It would be fully in the tradition of Padraig Pearse, whose centenary we celebrate this year; the patriot who did not shrink from accepting even "unconditional surrender" in order to prevent further slaughter of Irishmen.

I hasten to add that 1916 gives no kind of justification, provides no shred of excusation, for either the leaders, the men or the methods of those groups which abusively use up the name of the Republican Movement and the Republican Cause today. It is because they so frequently invoke 1916 and its leaders that I invoke for their reflection the example of those leaders. The ten-year old campaign of the present I.R.A. is now being continued, and can now be continued only, by methods repudiated by the men of 1916 themselves, the methods of "inhumanity and rapine". Their campaign is, so long as it continues, an insurmountable obstacle to any progress towards the United Ireland of which they speak. Their campaign has been and is the destruction of all the efforts made and the progress made towards reconciliation between the two divided communities in Northern Ireland. There is a verse inscribed on the historic bridge at Concord, Massachusetts, which recalls that in 1775 it was the English who fought "to keep the past upon its throne". In Ireland now it is the Provisional I.R.A. on the one hand, and the extremist Ulster Loyalists on the other hand, who are fighting and killing to keep the sectarian past upon its throne.

Appeal to republican consciences

One may be criticised in some quarters for acknowledging any elements of even distorted virtue among republican paramilitaries. But it is to their consciences which I am wishing to appeal. To make such an appeal, one must try to understand these men and their motivations. How can people come to feel that appalling deeds such as theirs are justified? How can one find a language which these men themselves, within their own special definitions of words, might understand, and which might lead them to reflect? I am trying to appeal to them in the name of the very values which, for them, constitute the content of the meaning of such words as "sincerity, idealism and nobility".

I appeal to their consciences. As a Bishop, as a priest, I appeal to them to repent. As a Bishop and as a priest, I make no one any apology for calling men to repentance; but I do not think that a call to consciences for repentance is truly such, or can be accepted by those to whom it is addressed as such, if it begins by assuming that these people are so morally reprobate that they have no conscience one can appeal to, and so are incapable of repentance. It would be a strange solution to violence which would be guilty of the very same moral obtuseness as we have noted in men of violence — that of "intense devaluation of the victim prior to action against him" (Milgram). Indeed, the very devaluation inherent in such terms as "psychopaths", "thugs", etc., could be used by some as pretext or justification for "brutal and inhuman treatment" of persons suspected of affiliation to such groups — as is clear from a study of the cases examined in the Compton and Bennett Reports and in the documentation of the Irish Government's case at Strasbourg.

Prayer for peace

In the last analysis, only God can touch consciences. Only God can bring us peace. Our greatest weapon, and our only infallible weapon for peace is prayer. Our prayer for peace must continue and must never slacken in its intensity and fervour. If we have been praying less frequently and less insistently for peace in the North and in the whole of Ireland, the events of Monday, 27 August 1979, in Mullaghmore and Warrenpoint will surely have impelled us to begin again and to pray harder. Our prayer for peace must be redoubled and must never slacken in its itensity and fervour. If we have grown weary of praying for this peace, then we must listen to Our Lord himself telling us to "continue to pray and never grow weary". If we had come to feel there was less need for prayer now, then we must recover our sense of urgency. When human efforts seem unavailing, we must remember Our Lord's words: "For men, this is impossible, but not for God:

to God all things are possible". The late Pope Paul, in his message for his last World Day of Prayer for Peace in 1978, reminded us:

> (Peace) is not ours; it comes down from the invisible kingdom, the kingdom of Heaven. We perceive its prophetic transcendence, which is not extinguished by our humble repetition of it: "Peace on earth to those on whom God's favour rests". Yes, we repeat: Peace must be! Peace is possible!. . . Peace is the gift offered to all people, which they can and must accept, and place at the summit of their lives, of their programmes, of their hopes and of their happiness.

Let that be our prayer and our programme, a programme for peace in Ireland, as we prepare, in this September of 1979, for the visit of Pope John Paul II to Ireland. Let the great prayer for peace of the People of God down the centuries, repeated often in the Church's liturgy, be ours today and every day:

> Yours, Lord, is the power, yours 'the sovereignty; you are exalted over all; give us peace in our time.

> Lord God, Creator of all things, awe-inspiring and strong, just and merciful, give us peace in our time.

7

SECURITY EXCESSES FUEL VIOLENCE

The need for security operations in Northern Ireland is incontestable, and should not be contested. The population in both communities should be willing to accept the unavoidable inconveniences which security entails, however irksome and frustrating these inconveniences, spread over so long a period, certainly are.

This being said, however, it is necessary that a number of points be kept in mind by those responsible for security. First, not every means for the elimination of violence is justified or is legitimate. Secondly, some of these means may merely produce short-term successes at the price of still more dangerous situations later on. Thirdly, violence in Northern Ireland is not the whole of the problem and the reduction or even the elimination of violence is not by itself the solution. To assume that security successes amount to a solution of the Northern Ireland problem would be to confuse symptom with disease. Violence in the North of Ireland is a symptom of a complex of underlying problems, and until these are resolutely and radically tackled, Northern Ireland will remain a chronically unstable and violence-oriented society.

Repression and the poor

I speak first of the means used to repress violence. The methods used for the repression of violence need constant scrutiny and appraisal. This matter cannot be left solely to the security authorities. These are naturally trained and predisposed to think in military terms, in terms of statistics of incidents and of casualties. No responsible person would question the importance of these considerations. But they are relevant to short-term pacification, and leave completely untouched the long-term reform of the society which is breeding the violence. What is worse, some measures of repression can actually increase the alienation and resentment of certain groups, can generate the kind of hopelessness which leads to fanaticism and can embitter a new generation and deliver them as ready-made recruits to revolutionary movements. Repressive measures indeed sometimes mirror the inherent injustices and inequalities existing in the society itself.

It surely should not pass without notice, for example, that the sector of the population which receives most attention and most severity from the security forces, the sector which provides most candidates for court sentences and for imprisonment, is the people from the small houses in the little crowded and unlovely streets. Surely we must be prepared to ask objectively whether some security policies might be alienating these people or leaving them open to the propaganda of the subversives. It is surely a matter for concern that security is seen by so many of these people as oppression. Whether they be Catholics or Protestants, the people most subject to security searches, house searches and interrogation tend to be from similar socio-economic and educational background.

They tend to be the people who "do not count in society"; the people whom the middle-classes can easily dub as "poor types", "up to no good anyhow". These are people with no "contacts higher up" to intervene for them, no one who "knows someone in the right quarters" to plead for release or leniency for them. Their conditions of life and their environment are mostly unknown to polite society. Their treatment arouses little resentment in influential society, because the people of the more select residential areas where "influential people" live do not know personally what it is to be harassed, house-searched and interrogated in this kind of way. Surely we must sometime begin to ask whether the fault is solely theirs, or whether it is society's too.

Some studies of crime and punishment in England have suggested that the severity of court sentences tends to bear some correlation with the socio-economic and educational background of the accused. Judges would seem, according to these studies, to tend to be more sympathetic with offenders from their own kind of background. There may be food for serious reflection by all of us here, and in the Republic as

well as in the North of Ireland. The Irish Bishops, in their
Pastoral Letter on justice, in 1977, declared that:

> it will hardly be claimed that, as things are now, a poor man's son
> has as much chance as a rich man's son of gaining his legal rights or
> of obtaining the law's leniency.

Those who try to take Christianity seriously must be particularly careful not to indentify the assumptions and attitudes
of their own socio-economic and educational class with the
Christian judgement of situations and of people.

The Irish Bishops' Pastoral called for urgent priority to be
given to national programmes for the reduction of unemployment and for the elimination of poverty. The Pastoral insisted
that unemployment and poverty were correlated with violence
in Northern Ireland. That insistence and that call must be
repeated today as part of our nation-wide "No" to violence.

Security and the law

The leaders of the four main Churches in Ireland recently
sounded a united note of concern about allegations of excesses
in security operations. Some of the reactions indicated that
there are people who seem to regard security as an absolute
end justifying the use of any means, provided only that the
means are effective. There are people who seem to treat
security operations as self-justifying and who regard any
criticism of the security forces as equivalent to support for
violence.

But security forces, precisely because they are society's
resistance to violence, have all the greater obligation to respect
justice and human rights. As the inter-Church report on
Violence in Ireland (page 75) put it:

> The danger of defence forces becoming step by step a means of
> systematic repression is a real one and the Churches could do the
> community a service by encouraging an impartial scrutiny of such
> possible developments.

Forces which claim to defend and restore law and order must
be seen to be amenable themselves to justice and to law. It
seems to be feared, by none more than the security authorites
themselves, that to make security personnel answerable to
the courts in cases of alleged infringement of human rights in

the course of security operations would undermine the credibility of the whole security operation and the morale of the security forces. On the contrary, it could go far towards strengthening their credibility and even morale. The inter-Church report already quoted continued:

> This (scrutiny) could be as good a protection for the forces against misrepresentation as for the public against abuse of power.

Some analogy may be drawn from recent American experience. It was a searing experience for the American soul to see the highest office in the land, with all the reverence and awe attaching to it, being made amenable to the probes and processes of justice; but the experience was therapeutic, penitential and purifying. It restored the dignity and saved the credibility of the American system of democracy at home and in the eyes of the world. Justice is its own reward; but it often brings nations other rewards in the shape of self-esteem, internal confidence and international credibility. There can be lessons for other nations here.

The British voice is rightly heard and must be further heard in protests against violations of human rights by governments and security forces in other countries. This desire of Britain to be the voice of justice for victims of repression in the world creates a need for special vigilance in respect of human rights and human dignity in her own security operations nearer home.

Boomerang effect of some security measures

Some current security practices in Northern Ireland seem likely to be sowing seeds of bitterness for a long future of grapes of wrath. Sometimes not only persons but names, family names and whole familites, seem to feature on security suspect-lists, occasionally even on the basis of what turns out to be false or malicious information, and people of that name or members of that family can apparently be subjected to an endless series of repeated security searches, interrogations, house-searches, etc.. Some innocent people have felt themselves almost hounded into membership of, or at least sympathy with, para-military organisations by endless repetitions of this kind of experience. It is in this kind of way that

the recruits for violence for future generations are pro-
grammed in the present. Can the vicious circle never be
broken? Must suspicion of violence necessarily be presumed
in the case of certain families, certain names, certain streets,
certain addresses? The habit of imputing "guilt-by-association"
is by no means confined to security forces. There is insult and
injustice in the use by journalists and by others of such terms
as "bandit territory", "notorious Border town", "infamous
Republican estate", to describe areas the vast majority of
whose inhabitants are law-abiding and peace-loving citizens.
This kind of language, with its almost quasi-racialist overtones, is no contribution to the cause of peace.

Armies are just not suited to civilian peace-keeping operations. Purely military thinking has a very restricted relevance
to civilian subversion. Security in this situation has as much
to do with a battle for minds, for credibility and for confidence, as with military successes. From these aspects, present army policies must be pronounced counter-productive.
Methods of interrogation are too often unjustifiably rough,
sometimes even brutal; the middle-of-the-night searches are
too frequent, too destructive, too often based on mistaken
identity; the language and the gestures of army personnel are
too often obscene and insulting; the signs of what can only
be described as a "Paddy-bashing" mentality are too frequent,
for one to remain silent about them.

What I am saying is not anti-British prejudice. It is not said
in anger. It is said in great sadness. It is said with regret and
with searching of conscience, for one is fully aware of the
danger of being misunderstood, of giving comfort to the
I.R.A.. But what I have said is said with moral concern,
for by such methods security forces do no eliminate men of
violence; they begin to resemble them. They do not crush
violence; they spread it. Such methods are providing a con-
stantly-renewed source of recruitment for the I.R.A..

The soldiers serving in Northern Ireland are not to blame
for all this. They are often bewildered and understandably
nervous youngsters, asked to do a desperately dangerous
and frankly impossible task. War is an ugly and brutalising
business. Urban guerilla war is perhaps even more ugly and
brutalising than "conventional" war. It brutalises subversives,
and it can brutalise regular soldiers too. But, surely, better

understanding of the situation, more enlightened briefing and leadership could be expected from the army commanders. Total political commitment to bring this sorry business to a speedy end by political action is morally owed as much to the soldiers as it is to the civilian population. But, while the security operation continues, surely, after ten years, there could have been more done to research and implement other than severely military forms of counter-insurgency.

Furthermore, the present practice of imprisonment, however different morally and distinct legally from the earlier policy of internment, seems in practice to be producing much the same result in the population from which the prisoners come. It used to be said that for every one interned person in the community, at least ten were embittered and alienated, if not left open to the propaganda of the groups of violence. Something quite similar could be said today.

In the whole are of security, it would seem that dogmatic and absolutist stances are unwise. The whole complex area of the philosophy of punishment, deterrence, re-education is involved. It is in general unwise to give security decisions and policies the character of matters of immutable principle, when they should surely be open to review in the light of their effectiveness and of their consequences in practice. What I have been saying is by no means a plea for softness towards subversives, many of them guilty of horrible crimes. I am merely saying that a system which serves to deepen alienation and to harden determination between two opposite sets of subversives should not be regarded as not open to discussion. It should not uncritically be presented and accepted as unqualified victory over subversion. It should not be forgotten either that clemency, responsibility applied, can also have a role in eliminating violence and in restoring respect for law.

The evil of violence

Lest anything I have said might be construed as condonation of the campaign of violence, I wish to reiterate in the most absolute terms the condemnation of violence which has been repeated over and over again by the Catholic Bishops over the past ten years. There was at no time and there is not now any moral justification whatever for the whole campaign that has been a plague on our country for the past ten years. Our experience in Ireland over the past decade verifies every line of the late Pope Paul's description of the effects of violence in his message for the World Peace Day of 1978. Pope Paul said:

> Violence is not courage. It is the explosion of a blind energy that degrades the person who gives in to it, lowering him from the rational level to the level of passion. And even when violence preserves a certain mastery of itself, it looks for ignoble ways of expressing itself: insidious attacks, surprise, physicaly supremacy over a weaker and perhaps defenceless adversary. It takes advantages of his surprise and terror and of its own madness; and if this is the relationship between the two contdners, which is the more despicable?

> As regards an aspect of violence that has been made into a system "for settling accounts": does not this violence have recourse to contemptible forms of hatred, rancour and enmity which imperil society and shame the community, in which they decompose the very sentiments of humanity that form the primary and essential fabric of any society . . .

> Violence is anti-social by reason of the very methods that allow it to be organised into group complicity, in which a conspiracy of silence forms the binding cement and the protective shield. A dishonouring sense of honour gives it a palliative of conscience. And this is one of the distortions, widespread today, of the true social sense, a distortion which clothes with secrecy and with the threat of pitiless revenge certain associated forms of collective selfishness. Violence distrusts normal legal processes and is always clever at evading the observance of those processes by devising, almost by force of circumstances, criminal undertakings that sometimes degenerate into acts of pitiless terrorism, the final result of a wrong choice of road and the cause of deplorable forms of repression. Violence leads to revolution, and revolution to the loss of freedom.

Irish experience corroborates every line of the Pope's utterance. It is the very vehemence of one's moral abhorrence of violence which provokes concern over policies which might serve unwittingly to prolong it and over claims which might engender complacency about the success of those policies.

The need for or the wisdom of a review of security policies may be stoutly or even heatedly denied, especially at a time when these policies seem to be working. But short-term effectiveness must be weighed against longer-term repercussions. In a security situation so complex, so deeply implicated with history and so politically intractable as that of Northern Ireland, security policies require enormous historical and psychological understanding, insight into the psychology of two frustrated and insecure working-class communities, great sympathy and flexibility. In the long run, security will operate successfully only when there is wide bi-community acceptance of and confidence in the security forces, engendered by acceptance of and confidence in the institutions which these forces safeguard. Security policies will ultimately succeed only insofar as they are accompanied by efforts towards a political solution.

This is not to say that security operations must be suspended pending political agreement. Obviously there must be security operations, there must be penalties commensurate with the grave crimes perpetrated and providing adequate deterrent effect. But let the wider aspects of the Northern Ireland problem be given equally urgent attention and receive equally sustained commitment.

The political vacuum

Over-shadowing the whole security situation is the absence of any progress towards the reform of the political process in Northern Ireland. Any security operation which is unaccompanied by movement towards a political settlement is condemned to long-term failure. Security without a minimum of political consensus and without promise of institutions commanding allegiance across the polarised communities inevitably comes to look like repression rather than restoration of political order. Some consensus regarding the institutions of law-making and law enforcement must accompany the necessary measures to restore the rule of law.

Direct rule seems to be becoming institutionalised and a certain complacency has been spreading about its merit and acceptability. Voices which are listened to with respect in Britain have argued that direct rule is the only policy which can in present circumstances command enough consensus to be viable. I believe that these voices are mistaken. I am convinced that the indefinite prolongation of direct rule will prove to be a grave error of judgement. Northern Ireland cannot be treated as though it were an English shire. It has a definite history, a specific historical and political experience, half-a-century's experience of a considerable measure of self-government. These factors cannot be treated as irrelevant. The place of Northern Ireland in the island of Ireland and its relationship with the rest of Ireland cannot be ignored.

In any case, suspension of the political process can never be good for people. It would be a strange judgement on the virtues of democracy to say that it could. Good and efficient administration is not substitute for a just democratic process. Paternalistic administration may hand down many benefits; but it cannot engender that sense of self-responsibility and that political maturity which are necessary if Northern Ireland is ever to become a stable society. The marginalising of politicians and the suspension of proper political processes have always been the recipe for future political and social violence.

The risks of a prolonged political vacuum seem to me to be very great. The first beneficiaries of the political vacuum are the subversives and their political activists. Without being alarmist, I suggest that one could easily dismiss these as politically inept and ineffectual. It would be more prudent to allow for a considerable level among them of political astuteness and ruthlessness and of expertise in the skills and techniques of political subversion. One shudders to think what the result of indefinitely prolonged years of future violence could be for the political situation in Northern Ireland itself and what its repercussions might be in the Republic of Ireland – even perhaps in Britain itself. In the absence of political institutions in Northern Ireland, it is subversion and violence which are becoming institutionalised.

Because of the continuing political vacuum in Northern Ireland, politicians tend to become marginalised and politics itself trivialised and discredited. The better political leaders are tempted to give up in frustration. Parties are menaced with dissension and fragmentation. Politics no longer attracts new men of ability and integrity. The beneficiaries waiting in the wings are the political extremists and ultimately the subversives. To speak only of the minority population, it seems to me that the massive willingness of this population to

enter into a normal political process, throught electoral support for constitutional political parties, marked an historic
turning point in the political aims and aspirations of the
Northern minority. This development should have been seen
and should now be seen as an opportunity, unprecedented in
the whole history of Northern Ireland, for the inauguration
of a new era of constructive politics in the North. This opportunity is being put at risk by the indefinite continuance of
political vacuum. A prolongation of sterile and self-destroying
immobility by some political parties, coinciding with, if not
taking advantage of, apparent inertia, or at least inaction, by
the British Government, could lead to the opportunity's being
lost. To miss the opportunity of constructive politics in
Northern Ireland, which has been made possible by the
development in question, would seem to me to be a political
blunder of great magnitude and an historic tragedy. All political parties would lose in such a tragedy: only subversives
would benefit and there would be no gain for any party and
only loss to divide among all parties opposed to subversion.

If ordered life in society depends upon the control and
distribution of power; if violence is power without responsible
control and without answerability for its use, whereas politics
is the rational and responsible control of power, then clearly
politics is the alternative to violence in society; and then,
equally surely, the elimination of violence requires the re-
establishment, *pari passu,* of the political process.

Politics the "No" to violence

Pope Paul invited us, as we entered 1978, to say "No" to
violence, "Yes" to peace. But he warned us in many mes-
sages in the past that peace does not come by merely wishing
it and violence does not go way by our merely condemning it.
We must create the politics of peace, we must build the institutions of justice, we must remedy the underlying situations
which lead to violence. In *Populorum Progressio* in 1967, just
before our tragic cycle of violence began, Pope Paul said:

> We want to be clearly understood: the present situation must be
> faced with courage and the injustices linked with it must be fought
> against and overcome. Development demands bold transformations,
> innovations that go deep. Urgent reforms should be undertaken with-

out delay. It is for each one to take his share in them with generosity, particularly those whose education, position and opportunities afford them wide scope for action (Par. 32).

In his 1978 message for peace, Pope Paul said, in words which, I suggest, have a startling relevance for our situation in Northern Ireland now:

Our war against war has not yet been won, and our "yes" to peace is rather something wished for than something real; for in many geographical and political situations which have not yet been settled in just and peaceful solutions the possibility of future conflicts remains endemic.

To say "No" to violence is to say "Yes" to the politics of justice and of peace. The implications for all political parties in Northern Ireland are clear. The inter-Church Working Party on Violence, appealed to all political parties in Northern Ireland to face up to the political logic of their rejection of violence and their commitment to peace. This Working Party, representing all the main Churches in Northern Ireland, said:

That all political leaders should be encouraged to see their task as that of reaching a just agreement with their opponents rather than of achieving victory over them; and that to this end they should be open to any reasonable settlement proposed.

That all people of goodwill should use their votes and their influence to encourage the politicians to see things that way.

This appeal needs to be made again, and with greater urgency than ever. It must be heard by all political parties in Northern Ireland, and especially by those who have made intransigence into a policy. Other subversives, I repeat, will benefit from the continuation of political intransigence and immobility and from the prolongation of the present vacuum.

8

THE POLITICAL VACUUM: BRITAIN'S OPPORTUNITY

People all over the world have, over the past ten years, been hearing and seeing news bulletins, commentaries and pictures, which speak of Protestants and Catholics at war with one another. Christians and non-Christians alike have listened, with astonishment and incredulity, to talk of "Catholic" guns and bombs or of "Protestant" guns and bombs; of "Catholic" and "Protestant" street-fights, rioting youths, barricades, private armies. Such language has been rightly thought incredible in this ecumenical age. It has constituted for many, in the most literal sense, a scandal, a stumbling-block to Christian evangelism and to ecumenical progress.

I have argued already that the situation is certainly not one of "religious war", and that the terms "Catholic" and "Protestant", are merely a convenient label for sociological communities, distinguished by a complex of differentiating features, among which the secular elements are more immediately relevant to the present violence than is the denominational one.

Unfortunate effects of partition

Very many other European countries had a similar history of religious division. Many countries have populations divided, like Ireland's, into two communities with different cultural, social, economic and political traditions correlated with the religious division. In nearly every other instance, however, a state of peaceful, and even creative consensus, or at least co-existence, has long ago been achieved. Unfortunately, the ill-conceived political solution imposed by Britain upon Ireland in 1921-1922 made this normal political development impossible in Ireland. The island was partitioned along roughly, though only approximatively, denominational lines. An area was cut off whose main indentification was that it contained the greatest concentration of Protestants in the island; although it also contained just as many Catholic-peopled areas as could be included with the Protestant areas without danger of ever reversing the Protestant majority. To this territory, Britain gave limited self-government with all the institutions of democracy.

The institutions and conventions established in Northern Ireland were, naturally enough, the British democratic conventions. The result of these was that a permanent majority of *de facto* Protestants had a complete monopoly of political power, with irremovable dominance over a permanent minority of Catholics. Meanwhile, in the rest of the island of Ireland, the population was composed, to a statistically overwhelming degree, of Catholics, and Protestants were a very small minority. The political philosophy of the independent State of the Republic of Ireland was, indeed, never a confessional or sectarian one. Its official commitment is to non-confessional republicanism. Identification with it was, to this extent, made easier for the Protestant minority. Furthermore, its political philosophy was, broadly speaking, shared by most of the Catholic community in Northern Ireland.

De facto, however, this republican philosophy was embraced as a political philosophy almost only by Catholics. It was given existence in terms of a political state by the struggle of Catholics. This struggle was first a struggle for religious emancipation against a politico-religious imperial establishment, before it became a struggle for political independence. This historical fact had inescapable consequences for Irish republicanism as it actually developed. Inevitably, this took on some of the external appearances of a confessional struggle, a struggle of Catholics for religious as well as for political freedom.

If the Catholic and the Protestant communities could have been sharing the island together under common political institutions, there would certainly have been movement towards peaceful and consensual cross-confessional political life. In other words, the processes which, in comparable situations elsewhere, led to the political transcendence of sectarian divisions, was inhibited in Ireland by the political partitioning of the island's population, which, in effect meant the political institutionalisation of the community divisions. The two political territories, and the two communities within the Northern territory, remained withdrawn in their respective areas, often feeding on one another's fears, suspicions, stereotypes, myths or ideologies.

Suspension of Stormont

The Unionist regime in Northern Ireland, associated with Stormont, failed to come to terms in time with the problem of an unreconciled political minority within its own territory. Instead of setting out to rally the minority to the institutions of the new State, it tended to develop what one might call a "Maginot-line" type of politics, cultivating defensive, protective and beleagured stances. Its policies, in many instances, seemed aimed at containment of the Catholic populations within their territories, as though to create confessional frontiers within the frontier of the State. During most of the history of the Stormont regime, housing policies were designed along confessional lines. The division between "Catholic" and "Protestant" districts did, of course, precede the political partition of the country; but the Northern administration made the reinforcement of the existing division, and its transference into new housing areas, part of its official housing policy during the greater part of Stormont's existence. The questions of "discrimination" and "denial of civil rights", are emotive and controversial. Nevertheless, the fact that there was discrimination in housing, in employment, in promotion, in educational opportunity, over the greater part of the history of the Northern Ireland administration, is well documented and cannot be dismissed. Indeed, a number of Protestant observers would now concede that abuses, in all of these areas, did indeed exist.

Nevertheless, when all this has been said, it must be clearly affirmed that it is unjust to describe the history of the North-Ireland state as merely "fifty years of Stormont misrule". Despite its failures, the Northern Ireland government achieved notable successes and accomplished progress in many fields, such as industrial development, education, health, social welfare, roads and communications, from which the Catholic population itself derived much benefit. Tolerance and inter-community contacts were, in fact, beginning to grow in the late 1950s and early 1960s. It was tragic that the Stormont administration misunderstood the true nature of the civil rights movement; and that this movement's demands for justice were misinterpreted as subversive, and that they were met by sectarian intransigence from loyalist extremists. It remains true that the Stormont regime failed in what should have been seen from the very beginning as its greatest single political task, namely winning the consensus of the minority community. Nevertheless, the Northern Ireland people have proved themselves capable of government. This is one of the great reasons why the present regime of direct rule is unsatisfactory and unacceptable.

Britain's historic responsibility

The Stormont regime had, therefore, serious inherent defects, defects which were ultimately to prove its own undoing. During the whole of the history of this regime, however, Westminster remained the sovereign government. It must be recorded, nevertheless, that the British Government, for the most part, evaded its responsibilities over internal matters within Northern Ireland. Indeed, a parliamentary convention was developed whereby questions regarding internal administration within Northern Ireland were dismissed at Westminster as belonging to the competence of the Northern Ireland Government, whereas challenges to the legitimacy of the Northern Ireland regime, or as to the justice of its internal administration, were equally dismissed as "interferences with the sovereign jurisdiction of the United Kingdom". The formula may have been convenient for Westminster ministers and politicians, but it caused intense frustration among those with legitimate and well-substantiated grievances. The price paid for these evasive stratagems has been extremely high. The tragedies of the past ten years have stemmed, in significant measure, from Britain's evasion of the Northern Ireland problem for the previous fifty. Britain has inherited from her own history and as a consequence of her own past political policies, an inescapable present responsibility for finding a solution to the Irish question. To extricate herself now from the situation which her own past policies helped to create will demand from Britain a degree of political insight, courage and resolution, which she has only rarely shown in her dealings with Ireland before.

But the Irish question now is one of the most serious problems Britain has on her hands. It weighs heavily on her domestic politics. The present commitment of the army in Northern Ireland is not only financially and psychologically oppressive; it has also the potential to create the serious hazards of the exertion of influence by military chiefs on political decisions. The Irish question weighs heavily also on Britain's European and world politics. A mere desire to withdraw from the Irish situation is no substitute for a real commitment to find and establish a viable solution. Until this is done, Britain will not even be able to withdraw from the situation.

"British withdrawal"

Responsible proposals have been put forward for Britain's "withdrawal" or "intent to withdraw" from Ireland. The language in which such proposals have been couched needs, however, to be very carefully parsed if simplistic and misleading interpretations of them are to be avoided. No responsible person believes that Britain could or should withdraw, in circumstances or conditions which would leave behind them in the North of Ireland civil strife, political anarchy or instability, and economic ruin. Such a situation would present an intolerable threat to the peace and political stability and to the democratic institutions of the rest of Ireland; it would be a situation which Britain could never tolerate, or be expeced to tolerate, on her own doorstep.

Another aspect of the problem, which has been carefully allowed for in the formulations of responsible calls for "British withdrawal", is the fact that the so-called "British presence" in Ireland is not only the presence of the British Army and of British organs of government. "British presence" is also a name for the presence in Ireland of something like one million people whose major community and political identification is their attachment to the link with the United Kingdom. I have strongly argued, in an earlier chapter, that this "British dimension", this "British presence", is an *internal* dimension of Northern Ireland reality. No responsible Irish man can or will either call for the "withdrawal" of this particular "British presence in Ireland", or give any countenance or condonation to any individual or group who would so call.

Responsible calls for "British withdrawal" are, therefore, I suggest, when properly understood, little more than calls that Britain should move, and move urgently, to devise and to secure acceptance for political institutions which will be free of the defects of the Stormont regime of the past, but still able to retain the loyalty of the Unionist and Loyalist majority, while winning that of the Nationalist minority. Then indeed Britain could "withdraw" in any sense other than that involved in and required by the rightful and permanent presence in Ireland of nearly a million people who think of themselves as British as well as Irish. There is perhaps little doubt but that if Britain would herself welcome "withdrawal" in circumstances such as I have described. It is hard to see how any responsible Irishman could wish for "British withdrawal" in any other sense, or in any other circumstances, than these.

Need for a political initiative

A political vacuum exists in Northern Ireland. It is in part a concomitant of direct rule. Direct rule does not positively facilitate the restoration of normal political processes. Indeed, direct rule, which was originally introduced as a temporary holding operation, intended to speed movement towards a political solution, has now negative effects in respect of such movement. There must be a new political initiative. This must come from Britain. It can come only from Britain. Such, boldly stated, is the case I wish to argue for here.

Direct rule has political anomalies and even constitutional absurdities of which few are aware. Northern Ireland is now ruled by a non-indigenous administration, none of whose members every had a vote cast for them in the area they govern. It is difficult for them to acquire knowledge of the psychology, history, traditions and cultures of Ulster, or to develop empathy with local feelings. This is no criticism of dedicated people who are doing their best. It is merely the facts of the situation.

Direct rule could be acceptable as an emergency measure of short duration, while political discussions were proceeding. Its indefinite prolongation in a political vacuum can only create what a Presbyterian Church document in 1972 called "a sense of pain and loss of confidence" among the people.

Powerlessness of local politicians

The current official line seems to be that the Northern Ireland political parties must "come together and work out a solution for themselves". But it must be observed that in Northern Ireland the political parties have no assembly for political debate, no Parliamentary Press Service to report their views to the public, and strictly no more rights than any citizen to initiate a public discussion. The former elected representatives in the outgoing Assembly and Convention have, in the present situation, no status other than that of ordinary citizen. It sounds incredible, but it is fact, that they have no official access to the Northern Ireland Office and no right to official information. Like any ordinary citizen they learn of decisions from the media. Like any man in the street they are left to infer or guess at official policy from events. How could politicians in such a situation avoid a sense of futility and hopelessness? How can political debate in Northern Ireland be other than unreal and irrelevant? In such a situation, extremist obstructionism is more important than political debate. Effective initiative passes into the hands of the sectarian demagogues — and of the paramilitaries. Insofar as these are consequences of direct rule, then direct rule is a recipe for alienation. In other words, the mood of alienation and exclusion which long characterised the minority community now risks being transmitted to the majority community too.

A healthy democracy demands participation of the governed. This is excluded by the present pattern of direct rule. The Northern Ireland Office is not accountable to the people whom it governs, since those people have no sort of representative assembly. The Office does not have to define or defend its policy decisions to those affected by them. Some sort of substitute for accountability to a debating Parliament could be provided by accountability to questioning journalists. But it is held by many that the degree of openness evinced even here leaves much to be desired. It will scarcely be seriously claimed that sufficient accountability is provided by the infrequent questioning and token Northern Ireland debates at Westminster. The degree of information, understanding or interest in Northern Irish affairs common in Westminster debates is, putting it mildly, not likely to dispel the sense of alienation and hopelessness in Northern Ireland itself. The corresponding debates at party conferences in Britain often engender something worse than hopelessness – namely, a sense of resentment.

The Sovereign Government

Yet, Westminster is the Sovereign Government. The Government's paper *The Future of Northern Ireland,* in 1972 (a paper which I have already called a landmark in British understanding and analysis of the Irish problem) has the words: "The United Kingdom Parliament must be the sovereign authority over all persons, matters and things in Ireland." Not only is the British Government the ultimate authority: it is in political terms the sole authority in Northern Ireland at this time. It would be disingenuous to pretend that the problem is an Irish one and the Irish must "settle it themselves". Even if – and this is a very large if – one were to leave history and even moral obligations out of it, one cannot ignore the constitutional fact and the political reality. There is no constitutional machinery, there are no instruments, no institutions available to Northern Ireland parties at this time for working out solutions.

The British Government did not leave the Scottish parties to work out formulae for devolved government in Scotland. Yet, under the existing constitutions and in the present political systems, Northern Ireland is as wholly and solely Britain's responsibility as is Scotland. Britain is not leaving the two Rhodesian communities to "work out their own solutions". Yet, Northern Ireland is much more directly Britain's historic, political and moral responsibility than is Rhodesia. Surely, Britain cannot with self-respect, with honour or with credibility among the nations, admit to political impotence and cluelessness at her own back door.

What can Britain do?

British readers may understandably ask, in genuine bafflement and frustration, if not with irritation: "But what more can Britain do?" It would be fair, but would be judged facile, to retort: "Do what governments exist to do. Assume the responsibilities of governing."

It will be more constructive to point out that Britain has had wide and usually successful experience in coping with analagous problems of constitution-making in overseas territories. Surely there are many models of constitutional conferences from which lessons can be derived.

Still nearer the point would be an in-depth analysis of why Sunningdale and the Assembly and power-sharing executive failed. There was, undoubtedly, exaggerated Sunningdale euphoria. There was unhelpful Irish post-Sunningdale triumphalism. But I am convinced that there has also been unjustified British post-Sunningdale pessimism. The failure was arguably due to factors which were avoidable and need not be recurring-accidents, mistiming (especially that of the United Kingdom elections), misinterpretation or misrepresentation (e.g. of the "Irish dimension"), an element of intimidation and propaganda during the U.W.C. strike, combined with lack of decisive British governmental leadership — perhaps even more than to majority Unionist rejection of the power-sharing principle. Sunningdale and the later Convention were something to learn from, to go forward from, not to despair over: above all, not to make a reason for opting out.

If much of the present malaise lies, and I believe it does, in the lack of seriousness in Northern Irish political discussion and the lack of official status by Northern Irish politicians, surely some new form of elective permanent constitutional conference chaired and convened by Britain, could be tried. It could have an open-ended mandate in terms of duration, to resolve any sense of threat or ultimatum by deadlines. It need have only the broadest of parameters, but they must be clearly defined and approved by Britain, the sovereign authority. Minimum conditions would surely be that any solution to be viable or to be accepted by Britain would have to recognise the bi-cultural community character of the population and embody elements capable of rallying the consensus of the majority in both communities.

This is obviously to stray beyond my competence as pastor and moral teacher. I make these points only because I could otherwise be accused of evading an obvious objection that there is nothing Britain can now do. What is within my competence is to say that I believe that the present policy vacuum and political inaction are morally intolerable. No one can guarantee the success of any new initiative. What is unpardonable is not to keep on actively trying. I believe that the new British Government must give early positive proof that it is re-thinking Britain's whole policy in respect of Northern Ireland and working towards a political settlement.

Economic deprivation

Britain's policy about Northern Ireland's economic future urgently needs to be clarified. For example, to what extent does Britain accept the principles of the Quigley Report? To what extent is she prepared financially to support its recommendations? Economic deprivation in Northern Ireland, as distinct from Britain, has close links with violence. It is unequally distributed. It is no accident that the areas from which I.R.A. militants operate are also areas of chronic economic and social deprivation and of endemic unemployment – the highest in Northern Ireland and perhaps the highest in Europe. Unemployed and alienated youngsters are a ready "teenage market" for the I.R.A.. A systematic policy of economic development in West Belfast and generally "West of the Bann" and in South Armagh, Tyrone and Fermanagh, would do much for peace.

It is most earnestly to be hoped that the new Conservative government will realise that economic reforms which they may judge beneficial in "mainland" Britain can have quite different, and potentially disastrous, results in Northen Ireland. Reductions in State spending in education, housing, social welfare, industrial and agricultural development, in Northern Ireland can have social consequences of a very dangerous kind. They can have repercussions on the continuance or intensification of violence which no government should risk. The correlation of unemployment and economic and social deprivation with violence is incontestable. No political or economic theory should obscure or override this fact.

Need for informed thinking about Ireland

Britain obviously cannot solve the Northern Ireland problem alone. The political parties in Northern Ireland have a
weighty responsibility. So also has the government of the Irish
Republic. If I speak mainly of Britain's responsibility, this is
not because I wish to minimise the responsibilities lying in
Northern Ireland and in the Republic.

The responsibilities and the obligations of the Government
of the Irish Republic are inescapable. But they are not always
objectively seen from this side of the Irish Sea. I suggest that
it would help in no small degree towards the search for a
solution to the Northern Ireland problem if British political
and media circles were to make more sustained and more
consistent efforts to understand political realities in Ireland
more accurately so as to be able to interpret political policies
and events and to assess political personalities in the Republic
more realistically. It is quite extraordinary, for example, that
there should have been so much misinterpretation in Britain
about the significance of the change of government in the last
Irish election. Specifically in its bearing on Northern Ireland
and on security, the significance of the change of government
was very widely and dangerously misread and the policies and
personalities of the new government commonly misinterpreted.
It is hard to explain and impossible to excuse this degree of
misinformation about Britain's nearest neighbour. This is only
one example; but it is a recent example and it is a glaring one.
There are many other examples of lack of information or
positive misinformation, and perhaps even more of lack of
empathetic understanding in Britain of Irish political realities.

The destinies and the well-being of these two islands have
been and are and will go on being too intertwined for this
situation to be tolerable. It is sometimes believed that Ireland
is riddled with anti-British prejudice. I do not honestly think
that this is so. Irish people in general like the English and ad-
mire many British traits and institutions. A million Irish-born
people live happily and contentedly in Britain and certainly
convey to their families and friends at home the opposite of
unfavourable reports or hostile attitudes about British people.
English visitors are welcomed and, I hope, made to feel they
are among friends when they visit Ireland. I really believe that
British history is more attentively and nowadays more objec-

tively studied in Irish schools than is Irish history in British schools. I believe that the Irish have more, and more accurate, information about contemporary Britain than the British have about contemporary Ireland. This is perhaps natural, because Britain is the dominant partner. But it is a situation with which no one should be satisfied and which should not be allowed to continue.

I believe there could be much more attention paid to Irish studies — historical, cultural, literary, sociological and political — in British education at all levels. I believe more and more British people should visit Ireland and see us for themselves. I believe that the few areas of prejudice or ignorance about Ireland which still remain in Britain should be recognised and should be treated. I believe determined efforts should be made to eliminate offensive so-called "Irish jokes", with their nasty racialist overtones. I believe editors and journalists should try harder to look objectively at Irish realities and be on the alert against deliberate or unconscious anti-Irish bias in their writing about Ireland. The quality press is usually well-informed, objective and fair. The popular press too often panders to vulgar and sometimes ugly anti-Irish prejudices. There is, happily, just no equivalent anti-British prejudice in Irish press coverage about Britain. We must come to know and to understand each other, because so many of our responsibilities are shared and because we have so much to gain from mutual respect and cooperation.

Bias and sometimes hysteria not infrequently occur in British media discussion of Irish security operations. Objectivity here should surely counsel moderation. The massive British military presence and intensive security precautions in Northern Ireland could not save the eighteen unfortunate soldiers slaughtered in Warrenpoint, just as Irish security failed to save Lord Mountbatten and his party on the very same day in Mullaghmore — though Irish security was able, within one day, and by a routine check, to apprehend suspects. In the very precincts of Parliament at Westminster, Mr Airey Neave met his brutal death, despite the intensive security appropriate to such a sacrosanct area; just as the British Ambassador to Ireland, Mr Ewart Biggs, was treacherously assassinated in Dublin despite Irish security precautions. Against Irish, as against international terrorism, there is no absolute security. What one of the greatest military commitments peace-time Britain has known cannot accomplish in Northern Ireland can scarcely be expected to be guaranteed by the Irish Army and Gardaí in the Republic. The bandying of taunts and sometimes insults about security across the Channel and across the Border is unhelpful and unjustified. Discussion about security should begin by Britain's full recognition of Irish good faith and unreserved commitment to the combatting of terrorism.

President de Valera made an historic broadcast to the Irish nation on 17 May 1945, at an emotional hour, following an unfortunate attack on Ireland in a victory speech by Mr Winston Churchill. The President expressed his hope for an Ireland ultimately reunited and reconciled in peace and by consent. He affirmed that it was not by violence that our ultimate unity and freedom would be achieved. He said:

> In latter years, I have had a vision of a nobler and better ending, both for our people and for the future of mankind . . . Meanwhile, even as a partitioned small nation we shall go on and strive to play our part in the world, continuing unswervingly to work for the cause of true freedom and for peace and understanding between all nations.

> As a community which has been mercifully spared from all the major sufferings . . . engendered by the present war, we shall endeavour to render thanks to God by playing a Christian part in helping, so far as a small nation can, some of the gaping wounds of suffering humanity.

May that be the noble vision of peace to which Irish and British politicians and people both dedicate themselves at the present hour. May this be the "nobler and better ending for both our people" to a history which binds us together inescapably; for one another's hurt and harm, if we do not determine that it shall instead be for each other's good.

9

PEACE IS MIGHTIER THAN THE BOMB

(Address for World Day of Peace 1979)

The late Pope Paul VI worked tirelessly, persistently and patiently during the whole of his fifteen-year pontificate for peace, peace between nations, peace within nations, peace in the hearts but also in the laws and institutions of men. In 1967 he launched the idea of a World Day of Peace, to be observed on New Year's Day each year. The first of these Days of Peace was 1 January 1968. Each year for the subsequent eleven years he endeavoured to prepare the Church and the world for this observance by a message addressed to Bishops and to all Catholics and to all "men of goodwill", developing one aspect after another of the overall concept of peace. He urged Bishops to organise liturgical celebrations, prayers, campaigns, educational programmes, in the cause of peace. He each year requested from each diocese in the world a report on the efforts which has been made in that diocese to observe the Day of Peace, and had a resumé published annually to record all the more important happenings and speeches.

Launching the series of World Days of Peace, on 8 December 1967, the late Pope strongly insisted that the peace he was striving to promote is not mere pacifism, is not a refusal of risk or sacrifice in the just defence of one's country, but "peace founded upon truth, justice, freedom and love". He kept emphasising, throughout the eleven years, the superior strength and commitment, the courage and the heroism of work for peace, by contrast with the hollow and lying bombast of propaganda for violence. He was serenely certain that:

> during the latest years of our century's history, it has finally become clearly evident that Peace is the only true direction of human progress (Message for 1 January 1968).

124

Pope Paul stressed the need for a clear-sighted awareness of the conditions and of the price of peace. In his first message for the first Day of Peace, in 1968, he said:

> Nor can one rightly speak of peace where no recognition or respect is given to its solid foundations: namely, sincerity, justice and love in the relations between states, and, within the limits of each nation, in the relations of citizens with each other and with their rulers; freedom of individuals and of peoples, in all its expressions, civic, cultural, moral, and religious; otherwise, it is not peace which will exist — even if, perchance, oppression is able to create the external appearance of order and legality — but an unceasing and unsuppressible growth of revolt and war.

"To reach peace, teach peace"

Shortly before his death, Pope Paul had defined the theme of the next Day of Peace. It was, "To reach peace, teach peace". Pope John Paul II endorsed this choice of theme and made it his own in his first annual message on peace for the Day of Peace of New Year's Day, 1979. With moving words, Pope John Paul says:

> I take from the hands of my revered predecessor the pilgrim's staff of peace. I am on the road, at your side, with the Gospel of peace. "Blessed are the peacemakers . . ."

Pope John Paul began his message by reflecting on the ineffectiveness and apparent hopelessness of the struggle for peace.

> In one place, timidity and the difficulty of carrying out needed reforms poisons relations between human groups in spite of their being united by a long or exemplary common history; new desires for power suggest recourse to the overpowering influence of sheer numbers or to brute force, in order to disentangle the situation, and this under the impotent and sometimes self-interested and compliant gaze of other countries, near or far; both the strongest and the weakest no longer place confidence in the patient procedures of peace.

Pope John Paul went on to spell out "a few elementary but firm principles", on which work for peace must be based.

> Human affairs must be dealt with humanely, not with violence. Tensions, rivalries and conflicts must be settled by reasonable

negotiations and not by force. Opposing ideologies must confront each other in a climate of dialogue and free discussion. The legitimate interests of particular groups must also take into account the legitimate interests of the other groups involved and of the demands of the higher common good. Recourse to arms cannot be considered the right means for settling conflicts. The inalienable human rights must be safeguarded in every circumstance. It is not permissible to kill in order to impose a solution.

The major theme of the papal message is, of course, education for peace. I shall refer later to some of the points made by the Pope in his reflections on this theme. Meanwhile, since the most urgent concern of Irishmen at this time must be the restoration of peace in the North of Ireland, I wish to offer some reflections on Pope John Paul's message and try to relate them to the present situation in Ireland, following ten long years of violence in the North. The words of the Pope which I have just quoted have an immediate and obvious relevance to this situation.

Ten years of violence in the North

The current violence in the North began, by a tragic coincidence, in the same year, 1968, in which Pope Paul launched his first Peace Day programme. It is possible now to review its results. I say without hesitation that there is a whole complex of evil results which can be directly traced to the campaign or campaigns of violence; and that there is no single positive good result which can be indisputably claimed to have been brought about by the violence. These ten years of violence have been lost and wasted years for all who have waged and all who have suffered violence. They have been tragically lost and wasted, blasted and twisted years for Ireland. If the course of Irish history has been or will be changed by the Northern violence, it will have been for the worse. It will take very many periods of ten years to undo the calamitous results.

The main sufferers have been the whole people of the North, the people of both communities; and almost certainly the community which has suffered most has been the Catholic community. They have been the most vulnerable to the economic and employment setbacks caused by violence. They have suffered most from the intimidation and enforced movement from their traditional neighbourhoods and homes which has been the form taken by loyalist counter-violence. This has been responsibly described as "the greatest single mass movement of population in Western Europe since World War II". This tragedy has had victims in both communities; but statistics show that it has predominantly affected the Catholic population. This has of course been an abhorrent injustice and evil; but it was an entirely predictable consequence of the I.R.A. campaign of violence, for it has been the age-old form always taken by loyalist violence.

There were no paramilitaries able to prevent this intimidation or to safeguard the exposed homes and neighbourhoods of Catholics in North or East Belfast. The result has been the decimation of adult and school populations in some of the oldest and staunchest Catholic parishes of Belfast, and a crowding of Catholics into over-crowded West Belfast. Thus violence, alleged to be for their liberation, has brought about for Catholics something very like the "containment" which Stormont tried to achieve but could never fully succeed in bringing about. Apart from those intimidated out of the neighbourhoods where they had lived for generations, as an indirect result of "liberationist" violence, hundreds more have been rendered homeless or have lost their livelihoods directly through "liberators'" bombs. I have been speaking mainly of Catholics, because it is Catholics primarily whom the Provisional I.R.A. claim to be defending and liberating; and certainly not because I am indifferent to the hardships and sufferings of Protestants. In both cases, it is the workers and the less privileged and less powerful members of both communities who are suffering most. In situations of violence, it is always the weakest who have the most suffering inflicted on them.

Violence purporting to be for the defence and uplifting of the working class has latterly mainly concentrated on the bombing of places of employment, means of transport, places of recreation, for the plain people of the North or, occasionally, of Britain. The violence of "liberators" has hit the plain people of the North, Protestant and Catholic, in their jobs, their ways of getting to work, their legitimate recreation. Their present homes, jobs and leisure hours are being destroyed; their future jobs and job prospects and their hopes of a better future for their children are being reduced to rubble.

When the North of Ireland is ultimately left to fend for itself, as it undoubtedly sooner or later will be, it will be next to impossible to find the resources necessary to repair the damage and rebuild the ruins. It will take at least a quarter century to recover the economic position we had reached before the violence began. The remaining and the extremely grave economic difficulties facing all Ireland at this time will have been rendered immeasurably more intractable. Continuance of this campaign of violence is suicidal. It is sheer political and economic madness. History will condemn it as anti-national crime. A resumption of the bombing in Britain would be a crime against the Irish who live there with their neighbours, as well as against the victims. It would be both sinful and insane.

The moral and spiritual damage

The worst consequences of the violence, however, have been moral and spiritual, rather than material. The foundation of all moral principle and the source of all human rights is absolute respect for the sacredness of human life. Incalculable damage has been done by violence to this sense of human life as sacred and inviolable. Human life is now made cheaper and more expendable than an armalite rifle. The horrifying crime of deliberate killing has become describable in the brutal and barbarous language of "a head job". Under the shadow of violence, crime and lawlessness have proliferated, and all kinds of immorality have been given an unprecedented chance to flourish. There is perhaps no greater single factor making for de-Christianisation and for irreligion in Ireland at this time than the campaign of violence.

In the Republic, once one of the most peaceful and crime-free countries to be found anywhere, violent crime has become a part of everyday life. Much of this has been an integral part of the paramilitary campaign in the North. More of it has spread by direct contagion from the violence in the North. If the Republic has now become an area of high incidence of violent crime, the leadership of the Provisional I.R.A. again bears a large part of the responsibility.

No future glory

Those engaged in planning or conducting violence may believe that their names will come to be written in glory, extolled in patriotic song and told in patriotic story. They are deluding themselves. History is not on their side. As Pope John Paul says: "Peace will be the last word of history."

Historians of the future will see the past decade as the decade which finally demonstrated for Irishmen the stupidity, the criminality, the futility, of violence as a solution to Ireland's present problems. This will, please God, be the one and only good positive result of the violence of the past ten years. It is a heavy price to pay for a lesson which should have been obvious before the campaign began. The paramilitary chapter of the past eleven years will be hopefully forgotten. What will be remembered will be the courage, the resilience, the cheerful doggedness with which countless thousands of ordinary people, Catholic and Protestant, have continued to live, to work, to hope and to smile and to forgive through these miserable years. What will be honoured will be the many hundreds of people who worked in spite of danger and antagonism for the welfare of the stricken, for reconciliation in and between communities, and for non-violent construction of a new Ireland.

Appeal to youth

One had fondly hoped that the leaders of the I.R.A. would come to see what dreadful damage to the quality of life their campaign was inflicting on the Ireland they profess to love. Such hopes have again and again proved sadly unfounded. These, however, are, for the most part, men of an older age group, men looking back to brood over ancient wrongs and nurse old resentments; not men looking forward with realism, vision and intelligence to a new Ireland of tolerance, reconciliation and partnership. They could still find a place in that New Ireland, if they could have the patriotism and the courage now to say, "Ten years is enough; we must give Ireland a different and a better chance". Otherwise they will have had their day, and it will have been a sad one. It must sorrowfully but honestly be confessed that the chances seem slim that they will listen to any appeals to desist from their disastrous and doomed campaign.

What one would have better grounds for hoping would be that the young people caught up in the paramilitary movement might have second thoughts about where they are being led. Could they not come to see that they are themselves being maimed as persons by their own guns and bombs? It does not come naturally to young people to kill. They have to be indoctrinated, brain-washed, made cynical, hard-faced and hard-hearted first. Something has to be killed in themselves first before they can kill others; and what is killed is what is most deeply human — compassion, sensitivity, humanity, what the older people called "nature". They should not continue to let their youth be stolen from them in this campaign.

They are being exploited. It is just as foolish for young Irishmen to let themselves be made bomb-fodder by revolutionary fanatics today as it was in the past for young Irishmen to cross the seas to become canon-fodder for imperialist war-lords. It was imperial generals and empire-building Colonel Blimps who, for their own purposes, created the myth of "the fighting Irish". It is pathetic to see young Irishmen today falling for that imperialist myth.

I wish to say to young people caught up in the revolutionary movement that no time is too late to come out of this spirit-destroying movement in which you are caught.

Come out before it mutilates your youth and cripples your manhood. Come out if you wish to be spared the anguish of a haunted mind, a tortured conscience. Come out unless you want to grow old hating yourself and nursing bitter memories of your ruined youth. Come out if you love Ireland and want to serve her. You belong to one of the finest generations of young people that Ireland has ever produced. Your place is with your own generation, building a new Ireland by their side, through your intelligence, your talents, your skills, your freedom from the myths and shibboleths of older men's rant and rhetoric. Nothing but your guns and the myth of the gun in which you have been indoctrinated are keeping you from joining with young people all over this country in building an Ireland better than our history has ever known. Otherwise, history will leave you behind, and you will be left, isolated and alone, to face a future of regret and remorse. Many have come out before you and have found a peace with God, with themselves and with their fellow-men which they had never previously known.

I fervently hope that young people may today listen to Pope John Paul's words:

> Young people, be builders of peace. . . . Resist the easy ways out which lull you into sad mediocrity; resist the sterile violence in which adults who are not at peace with themselves sometimes want to make use of you . . . You are the first victims of war, which breaks your ardour. You are the hope of peace.

"H-Block"

The Provisional I.R.A. have, however, by an extraordinary paradox, received great help from an unexpected source — the mistakes of the British administration and the security chiefs, mistakes in which they have persisted with quite remarkable obstinacy in the face of the lesson of all Anglo-Irish history and all experience. The I.R.A. was practically a spent and discredited force until they were handed the "H-Block" situation as a propaganda gift. This, and the unnecessary army harassment of innocent people, especially young people, among the "men of no property", are now

virtually the only source of vestigial sympathy or of recruitment for the I.R.A..

The I.R.A. are exploiting the H-Block situation with dis-
quieting success. In the United States in particular, where
the I.R.A. propaganda effort had been very effectively
neutralised, and the flow of money to them had largely dried
up, there has been a notable new recovery of lost ground and
a new upsurge of financial support on behalf of this organisation. This is due entirely to their clever and unscrupulous
manipulation of the "human rights" aspect of the H-Block
situation. This was entirely predictable and need not and
should not have been allowed to happen.

The first thing to say about this situation is that men are
suffering; men are suffering terrible degradation, in inhuman
conditions. Their families and friends are suffering with them
and for them. No matter what explanation or justification
is given for this situation, and no matter how responsibility
for it may be apportioned between the prisoners themselves
and the authorities, it must be declared that it is folly to
refuse to review the situation which allows prisoners to continue indefinitely living in such conditions. No matter how
the blame for the situation is apportioned, these conditions
are objectively in conflict with all recognised codes governing
the environment in which prisoners are to be allowed to live.
These conditions are in contradiction with all enlightened
contemporary penology. That the prisoners have chosen
these conditions and that their sufferings are self-inflicted is
partly true. This however is not a valid excuse for allowing
them to go on suffering. It is no justification for persisting
in security decisions which are proving to have results that
are both injurious to persons and self-defeating and counter-
productive in themselves.

Security decisions and policies should never be given the
absolute and immutable character of self-evident moral
principles. They must be constantly subject to review.
Policies which have as their main result let young men be
degraded and dehumanised inside the prison and provided
new recruits for the paramilitaries outside it, have surely
outlived their effectiveness and their credibility. These policies
surely can be changed. Saving political face should not stand
in the way; and surely many ways are conceivable, without

loss of principle, for bringing this situation to an end and thus depriving the I.R.A. and other paramilitaries of their last propaganda weapon.

There are times in history and in politics when gestures of clemency can be the catalyst facilitating a change of heart. Authority has to make itself admired, not just feared; it has to make itself wanted and valued, not merely reluctantly obeyed. Authority and justice themselves must be given a human face. Particularly when idealistic young people, however misguidedly and however culpably, become caught up in the net of violence, society cannot absolve itself from responsibility for the state of affairs which allows youthful idealism to be so corrupted and misled. It should not be impossible to find some imaginative formula which would enable the authorities, without sacrifice of principle, to "get off the H-Block hook", and yet not be seen to be surrendering to or condoning violence. Such a measure, at the appropriate time, could be an expression of our collective responsibility for what we all did and what we all fail to do in a society where young people are left at the mercy of evil circumstances which they did not create and emotional forces which they cannot control.

We are desperately in need of a change of heart in Northern Ireland. A change of heart cannot be forced; but it can be evoked. Only mercy can evoke mercy. Compassion cannot be compelled by force or fear; it can only be shown. By being shown, it justifies itself and indeed justifies justice. Clemency and mercy are not just Christian virtues. They can also be forces for political change and for social transformation.

There are political and legal implications in St Paul's analysis of the decadent state of Roman society in his time. He speaks to our condition, too, when he tells of men who have come to be "without honour, love or pity". He finds no escape from this "body of death", except in the "grace of God through Jesus Christ Our Lord". But, in Christian history, grace was a legal term, as well as a theological term. The grace of God, given to us through Jesus Christ, was held to call for answering human "grace" within the legal and penal system; and this because, to quote St Paul again, "we have all sinned and fallen short of the glory of God"; and can be justified only by the "free gift of God's grace".

It must, however, be clearly and emphatically stated that the exploitation of the sufferings of prisoners, the brave-sounding appeal to "human rights", emanating from the I.R.A. are disgusting. This movement has no right or title to invoke "human rights" for its immoral and anti-national campaign. Nothing that has been said by any of those sincerely concerned with human rights and prisoners' conditions carries the remotest implication of support for the I.R.A. or of approval for deeds of violence. No one who defends human rights could support or condone people who trample callously on the most sacred of all human rights, the right to life. Yet this does not make any less mistaken and foolish those who persist in enforcing security decisions which make it possible for this movement to wrap itself in the usurped mantle of human rights and justice.

The unacceptable political vacuum

It must also be said that the protracted political inertia of the British Government has contributed in a significant way to the prolonging of violence. Violence thrives in a political vacuum. Many in Britain seem to have become victims of the simplistic contention favoured by a section of their media that the conflict in Northern Ireland is either a religious war or else a peculiarly and eccentrically Irish problem; and that, in either hypothesis, the British Government has no responsibility or role in providing a solution. It cannot be too often repeated that Britain and Britain alone is the sovereign government, the only *de facto* government in Northern Ireland, and that the British Government is the only body which can take any political initiative or make any move in the direction of a solution. British national honour and historic justice demand that the British Government begin again, and soon, to face up to its responsibility to find a solution to the Irish problem.

Peace is the goal of history

We in Ireland should take to heart today the words of Pope John Paul II about the misreading of history which makes war and violence the salient facts of history and relegates to silence or to a secondary place the works and the products of peace. The Pope says:

> Let us first learn to re-read the history of peoples and of mankind, following outlines that are truer than those of the series of wars and revolutions. Admittedly the din of battle dominates history. But it is the respites from violence that have made possible the production of those lasting cultural works which give honour to mankind. Furthermore, any factors of life and progress that may have been found even in wars and revolutions were derived from aspirations of an order other than that of violence . . . Leaders of the peoples, learn to love peace by distinguishing in the great pages of your national histories and throwing into relief the example of your precedessors whose glory lay in giving growth to the fruits of peace: "Blessed are the Peacemakers."

We can thank God that the present teaching of history in Irish schools has already largely recovered the true sense of values desired by Pope John Paul. This sense of values must be communicated also to the wider public by all who have influence in society and have access to the media of communication.

Work and prayer for peace

Meanwhile, we in Ireland must do the works of peace and work to prove that peace works. We should be determined to refuse and to reject any solution of the Northern Irish problem which would be or would seem to be obtained by force or violence, by coercion of either community by the other, or by any means other than agreed mutual partnership between both communities in an Ireland where both traditions have equal citizenship and equal rights and opportunities. We must be convinced and must make our youth convinced that peace is the true love of Ireland, and that peaceful service of justice for all men and women in Ireland today is the true patriotism of our time.

This year we celebrate the centenary of the birth of Pádraig Pearse. May this commemoration be dedicated, not to the glorification of violence, but to the honouring of culture and the arts, to the advance of Irish education, to the promotion of social justice. Let us honour Pearse by "reddening with shame" that, in the words of his poem, so many of "the people that sorrow, that have no treasure but hope", still, in free Ireland, "have gone in want while others have been full". To burn with passion to end that situation, that is the task of the present generation of Irish men and women; that is the patriotism for young Ireland today; that is the "unfinished business" of 1916. That is the work of peace.

In the New Year now dawning we must all renew our fidelity to prayer for peace. Pope John Paul calls us to this today:

> Peace is our work, it calls for our courageous and united action. But it is inseparably and above all a gift of God: it requires our prayer. Christians must be in the first rank of those who pray daily for peace. They must also teach others to pray for peace. It will be their joy to pray with Mary the Queen of Peace.

Let us keep crying out every day to the Lord who bequeathed to us his peace: "Lamb of God, you take away the sins of the world, grant us peace."

We can have total confidence that he will hear our cry for peace, when we have prayed enough and worked enough to deserve it. Father Alfred Delp, a Jesuit priest executed by Hitler in February 1945, wrote these words just before Christmas 1944 as, in his prison cell, he calmly awaited death:

> Even this shambles in which we now live, this devastation swept by bitter winds of fate, is the destined place and hour of a new holy night, a new birth for humanity seeking God, a new nativity. Darkness will not frighten us or distress wear us out; we shall go on waiting, watching and praying until the star arises.

NORTHERN IRELAND: FROM IMPASSE TO INITIATIVE

(Address to the English Catholic Commission
for International Justice and Peace, London, 1 September 1979)

Speaking in London, within the week which has seen, in addition to the killing of a party of soldiers, the lamentable and ignoble killing of Lord Mountbatten of Burma and of members of his family in the course of their peaceful family holiday in Sligo, I can only say that Ireland is as stunned and pained and outraged by this deed, as the world stands aghast at it. As a Catholic Bishop, I wish to avail of this opportunity to express my sincere sympathy to the members of the Royal Family and to the people of Britain in their grief and bewilderment at this terrible deed. Lord Mountbatten was the bearer of a distinguished name, and had added further lustre to that name by his personal service to his country and to humanity. His place in British and in world history is assured. He won the esteem and even the affection of that great people, whose struggle for freedom was once inspired by Ireland's, the people of India, who have decreed seven days of national mourning for his death. It is tragic that such a life should have ended in this brutal way and that Ireland should have been the theatre for such an infamous deed.

It is with real anguish in the soul that one sees the depths to which political violence can descend. A group has claimed to have done this thing in the name of the Irish people. I can only say that the Irish people, in their immense majority, have repudiated and do repudiate, by every means open to them, all such groups and their sinister doings and subversive programmes. Indeed, I must add, that the Irish people are appalled and frightened at the Frankenstein of evil which has been set at large amongst them by the physical force movements. We can scarcely comprehend how men and youths of our own kindred can be brought to the point where such deeds can be calmly planned and coldly done without apparent qualm of conscience.

The essential evil of deeds such as this is that they violate one of the most sacred and fundamental principles of divine commandment and of moral conscience, namely that innocent human life is inviolable, and that any attack upon it is an offence against the majesty of God, whose image is reflected in the human person and whose divine Lordship is the guarantor of the sacredness of every human life. In this particular case, there has also been a violation of the sacred laws of hospitality, respect for which has been a proud boast of the Irish people throughout their history from the earliest times. Another cause for sorrow and shame in Ireland is that this deed has been done at a time when the whole Catholic people of Ireland are engaged in intensive spiritual preparation for the pastoral visit of Pope John Paul II. That this time should have been selected for this slaying of the innocent can only fill us with consternation that any group of Irishmen could be so much out of touch with the religious feelings of Irish Catholics at this time, and could bring themselves so to insult and outrage their spiritual sensibilities, as they await, in a spirit of prayerfulness and indeed of "national spiritual retreat", the coming of their Supreme Pastor. The nature and the timing of this deed are further evidence, if any were needed, of how foreign to the spirit and the traditions of the Irish people are the philosophy and the ethics and the tactics of those small groups of men who are committed to forcing political change by physical violence. Such philosophies may find mental and moral soul-fellows in the subterranean networks of international terrorism; but they find neither sympathy nor approval nor support among the vast majority of Irish people.

Ten years of sad experience have, however, borne home the lesson that moral denunciation and moral exhortation have very little effect upon people whose minds have been conditioned and whose moral sense has been perverted by the ideology and the ethics of violence. It is more important to try to analyse the factors which have brought this situation about and which serve to perpetuate it; and to examine yet again, but with renewed urgency, proposals which offer reasonable hope that the situations favouring violence might be remedied and the violence itself eventually transcended.

The present paper will argue for four theses in particular.

1. Violence in the North of Ireland has developed such effective strategies for military survival, and has sprouted tentacles clawing into so many departments of social life, that it constitutes a real danger to social and political stability in the whole of Ireland, and a potential threat to democratic institutions in Britain itself. To seek effective policies for ending it is a matter of national interest as well as of historic duty for Great Britain. It is also a matter of national urgency, requiring high priority among Britain's present political concerns.

2. The only effective answer to political violence is to create political institutions providing possibilities for non-violent social change and for peaceful movement towards a more just society.

3. Security policies should be subordinated to and should be at the service of clearly defined and resolutely pursued political aims.

4. The present policy of indefinitely prolonged direct rule is creating a climate conducive to the indefinite prolongation of violence; and it must be replaced urgently by new political thinking.

The new faces of violence

One can have some degree of sympathy with British spokesmen who might say that they have tried everything in Northern Ireland and can do no more, and that a solution cannot come from them, but must come from the local political representatives. If, however, this thinking were based on the assumption that time is automatically working in the long run on the side of consensus and of peace, or that the situation is anyhow improving as time passes, or that improved security can ultimately bring the violence under control, or that violence can be eliminated without political settlement and that, in any case, the basic problem is the violence, and politics must wait until the violence is first eliminated, then I fear that these assumptions will prove to be seriously and dangerously mistaken.

Over the past ten years, and at an accelerating rhythm

since the breakdown of Sunningdale and the fall of the Executive in 1974, the situation in Northern Ireland has deterior-
ated with every year that passed. The republican militarists
have not only acquired new sophistication in methods and
tactics of guerrilla warfare. They have not only arrived at a
high degree of efficiency in their techniques of survival. They
have not only become more coldly efficient and ruthless in
their definition and pursuit of 'targets'. They have also
mastered the grammar of international terrorism and im-
mersed themselves in its cluster of fanatical ideologies. They
have developed sinister links with international terrorist
organisations, and can rival many of these in sophistication
and "professionalism". We are not confronted any longer
with amateur, much less with armchair revolutionaries; but
with experienced and resourceful professionals. They boast
of their new professionalism; though killing is a profession to
which few would take pride in belonging.

The cadres of the activist republican groups have also become adept in the techniques of infiltrating many apparently
neutral sectors of community life. They have built up complex networks of business interests. Despite a professed ideological detestation of capitalism, they have extended tentacles
into trade and commerce, the property market, housing allocation, the illegal drink trade, transport operations. Some ob-
scurity still surrounds a recent find in the Republic of a huge
drug-smuggling operation; but that this should be shown to
have links with subversive groups would be completely in
character with their other known activities. All this is in addition to the various forms of "protection racket", which have
been a long-standing feature of I.R.A., U.D.A. and U.V.F.
groups in the North of Ireland. Such activities, apart from
being a very lucrative source of funds for the subversive
organisations, also enable them to burrow deep into the
fabric of communities. Its systematic infiltration into so
many of the patterns of community relationships makes subversive violence very difficult to eradicate from a community
into which it has pushed its roots. Such activities make it
hard to demarcate subversive crime from non-political crime,
and make the detection and elimination of either form of
crime immensely difficult. It is impossible to say, for example, how much of the epidemic of bank raids, which we

have had over recent years in both parts of Ireland, is traceable to "ordinary" criminals, and how much to subversives; or indeed how much might be due to a sinister compact between the two.

It could easily be foretold, many years ago, that subversive violence could not long be contained within the territory of Northern Ireland. It was both geographically unavoidable and politically predictable that it would "spill over" into the Republic. This has happened to a disturbing degree. The republican movements are as much committed to the subversion of the democratic institutions of the Republic of Ireland as they are to the institutions of what they choose to call "British rule" in Northern Ireland. Their language regarding the political institutions of what, in common with loyalist bigots, they call "the Free State", is as vitriolic as that which they use about British institutions. At the present time, counter-subversive security measures are costing the citizens of the Republic of Ireland proportionately more per capita than even the enormous cost to British taxpayers of security in Northern Ireland. This, by the way, is an interesting commentary on the claim, of which sometimes one still hears echoes, that the Republic of Ireland has no business "interfering in the affairs of the United Kingdom". Neither the United Kingdom, with its immense commitment of men and resources to Northern Ireland security, nor the Republic, with its relatively massive security commitments, can claim great success in counter-terrorist operations. This should temper accusations of security failure in the Republic.

The longer this situation continues, the greater the risk to peace and order in the Republic of Ireland, if not, indeed, to these islands as a whole. I fear that the long-drawn-out continuance of political violence in the North, if conjoined with economic difficulties, unemployment, particularly youth unemployment, and inflation in the Republic, could constitute a combination which would be full of danger to social and political stability and to democratic institutions all over Ireland. The Irish Bishops, in their Pastoral on Justice in 1977, warned about the "very great dangers of grave social and socio-political tension", which could ensue from failure

to face the challenges of unemployment and social justice in
the present situation in Ireland.

It is therefore, time that the politicians in Britain gave up
any illusion that the Northern Ireland problem can safely be
left to "sort itself out", or that it can safely be postponed
until urgent domestic problems regarding the economy, etc.,
can be solved.

A religious conflict?

Several recent commentators on the treatment of the
Northern Ireland conflict in the British media have deplored
the absence of analysis of the situation, and the facile recourse
to such simplistic formulae as that of "religious war". I have
discussed this question earlier. This terminology is, at most, a
half-truth, which can be convenient to politicians in the short
term, but which can be highly dangerous in the long run by
diverting attention from the political aspects of the conflict.
I would argue that the use of the terms "Protestant" and
"Catholic" to describe the parties in conflict has become so
unhelpful as to be positively an obstacle to objective analysis
and to the search for a solution.

The use of religious terms obscures the issue. These terms
describe sociological groups which historically have had, and
which continue to have, many distinct and even opposing
features. One of these is indeed religious denomination. But
there are many others, including economic, social, cultural
and political features. The cultural, socio-economic and
political features have much more relevance to the present
conflict than has the denominational affiliation. Solutions to
the conflict must be sought in these areas. The relevance of
the strictly religious factor is marginal, rather than central.
The effect upon the violence of strictly religious activity, in
the sense of ecumenical dialogue and efforts towards denominational reconciliation, is limited. Such activities are good
and necessary in themselves. They are an imperious Christian
duty for all the Churches. But they neither have nor can have
a decisive impact on the actual violence. What the Churches
can do to "solve" the problems of violence is extremely cir-
cumscribed. Indeed, it has been humbling for Irish churchmen, over the past ten years, to be brought face-to-face with

their relative powerlessness in situations of armed conflict.

One consequence of seeing the Northern Ireland problem in religious terms has been the appeal to such remedies as that of "integrated schooling". I do not propose to discuss that complex issue here. I merely wish to refer to some conclusions of James Russell, who has to his credit an impressive body of research into this whole question. He recounts that he came to Northern Ireland in the 1960s, sharing "the popular assumption that separate schooling for Protestants and Catholics leads to, or at least reinforces, discord, disorder and consequent violence". He expected research to confirm this assumption. Instead, his research convinced him that this hypothesis is at variance with the facts. He concluded that it even distracts attention from the real causes of discord and the real directions along which solutions must be sought. He declares that only "the existence of a political institution which is generally accepted as fair and impartial" will produce the desired change in community attitudes (cf. above, p. 25).

It is my conviction (and here I do not attribute these views to Russell) that resentments in the minority community derive from its half-century experience of being excluded from the decision-making processes of government. This inevitably fosters a sense of alienation, of not belonging, of being "against the Government", "against the Establishment" One does not have to be a social psychologist to realise that such an experience creates very serious obstacles to the development of a sense of identification with the institutions of government. This is basically a political problem, for which the solutions have to be political.

John White has studied several nineteenth-century situations of apparently "sectarian" conflict, which have analogies to the Northern Ireland situation. He finds these situations in various British cities, as well as in urban areas in the United States and in Germany and in Austria. In each of these cases, there was an economic and social and political aspect as well as a religious aspect to the conflict. A Protestant workforce, or, as the case might be, a Catholic ascendancy, felt threatened in its economic or employment security or in its political stability by a religious minority. In every single case, however, as White shows, the sectarian conflict was resolved; resolved, however, not by theological discussion and not by ecumenical activity, but rather by political development and socio-economic progress. The solution in every case came from movement towards a political situation in which the denominational minority could participate in the political process, and thereby acquire both some degree of political power and a sense of political responsibility. I believe that this analysis is extremely relevant to the Northern Ireland situation.

Politics and justice

Churchmen have their responsibilities. We must not attempt to deny them. I hope we will not shirk them. But churchmen cannot deliver solutions to the questions I have been discussing; and these questions are basic to the whole Northern Ireland problem. Political questions must be given political solutions.

Any objective analysis of the Northern Ireland situation must begin by recognising that there exist two historic communities in Northern Ireland, which are differentiated by their diverse understandings of history, their contrasting experiences of access to power and privilege and opportunity. These are not matters of abstract theorising. They have had very positive results, in the contrasting socio-economic profile of both communities, in terms of job-prospect, average size of income, distribution of income-groups over the population — as the figures from the recent report from the Fair Employment Commission placed beyond argument.

In the concrete Northern Ireland situation, I am convinced that justice as between the two historic communities requires that representatives of the minority community be given proportionate but real access to the levels where the political decisions are taken which determine the distribution of power and wealth and opportunity, the allocation of industries, resources and jobs. It is a matter for political discussion and negotiation how this can be brought about. Whatever means be adopted, there will be no inherent reason requiring that this arrangement be permanent. But only some effective machinery of this kind will create a possibility for political movement, there can be no escape for either community from the vicious spiral of violence.

John White has argued that the alleviation of sectarian conflict in other countries has come about only when "one or other group of politicians found it in their interest to build a coalition cutting across denominational boundaries". There can be no beginning of movement in that direction until, to start with, representatives of the minority community have a real prospect of participation in real political power.

I repeat that the ways in which this sharing of political power can be brought about are political questions in which, as a churchman, I have no competence. But I must say firmly as a Bishop that I believe this sharing of access to political power is itself a matter of justice transcending politics.

If anyone doubts this, let him think seriously about the effects on a whole community of its being regarded as unfit to be trusted to exercise power responsibly, as incapable of sharing effectively and responsibly in the government of its homeland. Surely this constitutes a manifest affront to human dignity, a clear denial of political justice.

A relevant British analysis

I have already referred to the British Government's own analysis of the Northern Ireland problem in the Green Paper of October 1972. A new Conservative administration could well take this document as point of departure for a fresh initiative now, seven years later. This document recognised that the essence of the Northern Ireland problem is that there are two communities in Northern Ireland, whose radically different historical, political, and indeed national traditions excluded the very consensus on fundamental political issues which are the normal and the necessary presupposition of a democratic State. The document states:

> The special feature of the Northern Ireland situation was that the great divide in political life was not between different viewpoints on such matters as the allocation of resources and the determination of priorities, but between two whole communities.

This analysis led the then British Government to the conclusion that:

> The two primary purposes of any new institutions must be first to seek a much wider consensus than has hitherto existed; and second

to be such as will work efficiently and will be capable of providing the concrete results of good government: peace and order, physical development, social and economic progress. This is fundamental because Northern Ireland's problems flow not just from a clash of national aspirations or from friction between the communities, but also from social and economic conditions such as inadequate housing and unemployment . . .

A Northern Ireland assembly or authority must be capable of involving all its members constructively in ways which satisfy them and those they represent that the whole community has a part to play in the government of the Province. As a minimum this would involve assuring minority groups of an effective voice and a real influence; but there are strong arguments that the objective of real participation should be achieved by giving minority interests a share in the exercise of executive power . . .

There must be an assurance, built into any new structures, that there will be absolute fairness and equality of opportunity for all. The future administration of Northern Ireland must be seen to be completely even-handed both in law and in fact.

Everything that has happened since has demonstrated beyond any possibility of doubt that it is only along lines such as these that any acceptable solution, with any hope of laying foundations for lasting peace, can be based. In a situation in which there are, within the same territory, two communities, with two radically different conceptions of what would be, from each of their points of view, a viable solution, there must obviously be an ultimate arbitrator or guarantor whose decisions and limiting conditions must be final. In any case, the Northern Ireland territory has never been nor seen itself as being an autonomous entity with a sovereign parliament. It cannot and should not be expected to take sovereign decisions.

Furthermore, each community has traditionally looked beyond itself for the source of its identity and the goal of its aspirations. One community has as its most cherished heritage a British dimension; the other has as its most characteristic identification an Irish dimension. For either of the two governments envisaged in these dimensions to say that it is "a problem for the people of Northern Ireland to solve for themselves", would be an abdication of responsibility and a refusal to recognise the realities of the problem. There is a British dimension and an Irish dimension in Ulster politics; and they can neither of them be dismissed as importations from outside, or as alien to the situation and able to be eliminated from its solution. An Irish dimension, just as much as a British one, is an internal dimension of the Ulster political problem; and any viable solution must give recognition to it. Equally, there is a Northern Ireland dimension in Irish politics, and it also is an internal not an external problem.

Finally, the Irish problem is a problem of domestic politics for Britain; and it deserves and needs the commitment of the best political brains which Britain has at her disposal at the present time. It is Britain which, in the last analysis, must determine the parameters of a solution; and must, with impartial justice and at the same time with firmness and finality, convince both communities that these ultimate parameters are the conditions governing further elections and consultations. Statesmen have, after all, a duty to lead and not only to consult. There are situations in which a community may not even know "the things which are for its peace"; and it is the duty of those who bear the ultimate responsibility for peace to confront them with the realities of "the time of their visitation".

The term, "power-sharing", may have become emotive, as much as descriptive. Its descriptive content may have become distorted or diluted by over-use. But the reality behind the term retains all its relevance in the search for a political solution. Both major parties in Britain have so far retained and frequently reaffirmed their commitment to some form of real sharing of power between the communities in Northern Ireland. I trust that politicians and the general public in Britain realise the extreme gravity of the implication of any suggestion of an abandonment of that commitment, whether overtly or by a device which would retain the words, but evacuate the content. The disastrous situation in Northern Ireland calls, and calls urgently, for new movement towards a political settlement embodying political justice and equality of rights, with accompanying equality of responsibilities, for both communities.

Security policies

Meanwhile, there is, alas, the terrible reality of the continuing violence. An ill-conceived phrase was once put into circulation, that of "an acceptable level of violence". There is not such thing as an "acceptable level" of murders. There is no acceptable level of such crimes as that committed on 27 August in a holiday boat off the Irish coast at Mullaghmore. Security is an inescapable necessity. The present week is not a propitious time to make the case that certain security policies not only do not contain or reduce the violence, but actually serve to fuel it. Of this, however, I am profoundly convinced; and it is my very abhorrence of violence which constrains me to question several aspects of security policies in Northern Ireland.

The first thing I wish to say is that the Northern Ireland problem is much more than a security problem, and security successes alone will never solve the problem. The elimination of violence would indeed be a mighty achievement, bringing unqualified relief to both Northern Ireland communities. But, even if the present violence were completly eliminated, Northern Ireland would remain a chronically politically unstable and violence-prone society, unless the root causes of the violence were firmly tackled, and unless the political structures of a just society, recognised and accepted as such by the majority of people in both communities, were established. Those concerned about peace in Ireland should be vigilant about any presentation of the problem as merely a security problem, or one susceptible of military settlement.

Secondly, security decisions and policies should be open to review and should never be given the status of inflexible principle. Moral detestation of and just retribution for proven crimes are one thing — and there is unquestionable need for both in Northern Ireland, where crimes have been horrible and guilt has been undeniable, and has often been fully proven. But those who determine security policies must be concerned also about their practical effectiveness in achieving their aims, namely the elimination of violence. If it were found that, on the contrary, certain security policies merely extend the range of alienation and resentment; if it were found that certain policies merely increase the flow of recruits into subversive organisations; if it were found that certain security policies merely created conditions for the deeper and longer indoctrination of prisoners into the ideology and methodology of subversion, then surely the policies in question should be suspected to be counter-productive and should be reviewed. Security policies can serve merely to recycle violence, rather than to eliminate it.

I believe that there have been mistakes and excesses in security policies; and that many of these can be traced to the conviction that the Northern Ireland problem is primarily a security problem, to be solved by security measures. In a recent sociological study of "struggles in a Belfast community", entitled *The Policies of Legitimacy,* Frank Burton remarks:

> The threat that national and international political violence poses, both to governments and to potential victims, has generated a widespread concern with the nature of political violence. Most of this concern . . . has taken the form of an interest in counter-insurgency techniques. The practical interest in combatting "terrorism" has relegated the explanation of its origin and forms to a secondary position. Indeed, the very attempt to explain the incidence of any particular form of political violence is liable to be branded by, for example, counter-insurgents as the propaganda of sympathisers. Politicised violence is, however, too important a social phenomenon to be left to the theorists of social control. [The author instances Kitson, Clutterbuck, and Moss.]

It should surely be possible, after ten years, to have devised security policies which would be as little oppressive as possible to peaceful and law-abiding people in their streets and in their homes, and would be less likely to alienate people who have neither association nor sympathy with terrorists. It should be possible to avoid, or to extricate oneself from, policies which are easily exploited by terrorists for their propaganda purposes. It is only plain fact to state that, as things now are, the British Army and the security forces are not believed, not trusted, not accepted, in many Catholic areas; and this in spite of the sincere abhorrence, among nearly all the inhabitants in those areas, of men and deeds of violence. Any army or security chiefs anywhere, finding themselves, after ten years presence, in such a posture, would surely begin to ask themselves some searching questions.

The third thing I wish to say in this connection is that security policies and practices, like all human affairs, are subject to the moral law of respect for human rights and human dignity. This sounds a platitude; but it can be over-

looked, because we all grant presumptions in favour of our
own armies and police forces, and the institutions and processes which they serve. These presumptions are often justified. But they are not automatically just. It takes a deliberate
effort from all of us to surmount the "idols of our tribe"
and to be objective about the "sacred cows" of our nation.

The subject of torture or degrading treatment is emotionally
explosive, where the security forces of our own country are
concerned. We must, however, try to triumph over emotion
by moral reason and conscience. On this question, I shall only
say that a dispassionate reading of the Compton, Gardiner and
Bennett Reports shows that abuses did exist, that abuses are
always possible, and that moral vigilance over security policies
is necessary. Counter-insurgency is not an absolute beyond the
moral law. It is always so much more easy to recognise security
excesses in far-off lands than to recognise them in our own.
But the Christian cannot evade the duty of moral vigilance,
or forget the Lord's injunction about the visual block in one's
own eye.

The political vacuum
The present Northern Ireland regime of "direct rule" from
Westminster was first introduced as a short-term and strictly
interim provision, which was intended to create the context
for rapid movement towards new political structures. It was
not originally intended to be in itself a political answer to
Northern Ireland's problems. Its indefinite prolongation, in
the absence of any political policy, has proved to have consequences quite contradictory of the original intention. Direct
rule has become an obstacle to movement towards a political
solution. To have allowed the policy of the Green Paper of
1972, and the ensuing Constitutional Proposals of 1973, to
fall in ruin, and to have done nothing since to rebuild on the
ruins, is a serious abdication of political responsibility. The
political vacuum which exists in Northern Ireland today is
unpardonable, and it is disastrous. If revolutionaries be fish
that need suitable water in which to swim, then that water
at this time is not so much sympathy in the ghettos as the
messy mix of direct rule, security methods without apparent
political policy, and total lack of political initiative.

Direct rule means the suspension of local politics, the absence of seriousness in local discussion of politics, the lack of any credible political alternative to the violence. When there is not official forum for political debate, parties fragment, the best lose interest and opt our, the worst intrigue and obstruct with passionate intensity. Politicians are off-staged by paramilitaries. Politics become discredited, all initiative is given over to men of violence. Security measures alienate the innocent and leave them open to exploitation by the paramilitaries. The absence of political iniatiative on the part of the administration combines with the other elements to generate in people a sense of hopelessness. It is even more true towards the end of 1979 than it was when the Northern Catholic Bishops first said it in 1971:

> Far-reaching political initiatives must be sought as a matter of great urgency if those who advocate violence are to be deprived of their chief ally — despair.

There must now be movement beyond and out of the present impasse. I shall quote again from the Government Green Paper:

> It can be argued that the British democratic system only works where a regular alternation of parties is possible; that the real test of a democratic system is its ability to provide peaceful and orderly government and that by that standard the existing system has failed in Northern Ireland; that other countries with divided communities have made their special constitutional provision to ensure participation by all; that a number of these countries have had stable and successful coalition governments over many years; and that there is no hope of binding the minority to the support of new political arrangements in Northern Ireland unless they are admitted to active participation in any new structures.

The British Government itself solemnly warned in 1974 that, if its Constitutional Proposals were rejected or frustrated, disaster would follow. It declared:

> They can be frustrated if interests in Northern Ireland refuse to allow them to be tried, or if any one of the communities is determined to impose its will on another. It should now be perfectly clear that these are prescriptions for disaster. The Government believes, however, that the majority of the people of Northern Ireland have an overwhelming desire for peace and that they will accept the opportunity which these proposals utter.

The fruits of peace

It is an under-statement to say that the restoration of peace and stability in Northern Ireland will not be easy or rapid. A will to cooperate between all those concerned in the complex tragedy is required. The Northern Ireland political parties, the Government and the Opposition in Britain, the Government and the Opposition in the Republic, all have their part to play, their obligations to accept. I speak only of the political agents. I am not forgetting the Churches. We too have our distinct but inescapable obligations, and we shall not shirk them.

The difficulties are immense. But the fruits of success are incalculable. It would indeed be rash to underestimate the risks for all of us in these islands of not finding solutions for the Northern Ireland problem. But, on the other hand, it would be difficult to exaggerate the benefits for all of us which would flow from bringing about a peaceful and just and reconciled society in Northern Ireland.

If Britain were to set herself with enlightenment, determination and courage to find a solution to the Irish problem, the goodwill generated thereby in her neighbouring island and among the Irish diaspora all over the world would be a political asset of very considerable importance, and would enhance Britain's credibility and influence as a force for peace and reconciliation and justice in the world. The exemplary significance for Europe and for the world of the settlement of a problem so deeply rooted in history as the Irish problem, would be of historic significance and would be of considerable international political importance.

The history of Anglo-Irish relations has not always been a happy one. One consoling fact emerges, however, from that history; namely that, when relations between our two peoples are established on a basis of equality of rights, of dignity and of reciprocal respect, then a spontaneous friendship and even affinity between our two peoples asserts itself. The British politician who shall have set himself the task of achieving peace in Northern Ireland, and thereby permanent peace and friendship between our two islands, would have an honoured place in history. To work for this, on both sides of the Irish channel, could be our most appropriate joint monument to the memory of the late Lord Mountbatten of Burma.

Reconciliation

I shall end by one word to myself and to my brother-churchmen. We are prone to preacher's words and preacher's attitudes. We easily appear as sentimentalists, romatics, other-worldlings, abounding in a rhetoric remote from reality and using words which disguise the all-too-human stuff of men and of society.

We preach reconciliation; but we seem often to mean by it that some words are to be spoken, some gestures are to be performed, but that nothing actually has to be changed, no one actually has to change. But reconciliation is not verbal formulae or ritual gestures. Reconciliation is change: its meaning is *in* the changes that actually happen. Reconciliation in Northern Ireland will begin to happen, not when Protestant and Catholic churchmen walk arm in arm down our Royal Avenue in Belfast; but when structures of political partnership are functioning, when barriers to opportunity are removed on both sides, when avenues of employment are open to all, when disparities of wealth and privilege between communities are reduced, when human dignity is accorded equal rights and equal respect, regardless of address or school or church or chapel. The gestures can happen then; because only then will they be sincere. Before that has happened, they might be only clerical games.

What I am saying is not some social horizontalism substituted for the gospel of Jesus Christ. What I am saying is basic Christianity. It is gospel truth. I have been merely spelling out the meaning of conversion, of *metanoia*. Men have to change, change themselves radically, before their repentance is real. The test whether they have changed is to be found in what they do, more than in what they say. It is to be found in the structures of their society more than in their feelings of generalised benevolence.

We have a command of the Lord to establish reconciled structures and exercise reconciled behaviour, rather than merely cultivate feelings of reconciliation. This is made by the Lord a test of faith itself, when he says: "Repent and believe the Gospel." This is how we have to "redeem the time" before Christ comes again; for he comes quickly (*Apocalypse* 22:20).

LETTER TO A NORTHERN IRELAND PROTESTANT

One of today's popular Christian hymns says: "You will know that we are Christians by our love." You and I could scarcely claim that our communities have always measured up to that sentiment in our relations with one another. But, through the great grace of the ecumenical movement in all our Churches, we have come to know each other better and to understand each other's beliefs more accurately and more sympathetically.

One especially happy result of the ecumenical progress of recent decades is that we can accept each other as we are, in our differences. A Catholic can thank God for those Christian values and that Christian witness, which he admires in Protestants. A Protestant for his part can, we hope, do the same in respect of Catholics.

Northern Protestants
For my part, I can only put on record my sense of admiration for the Christian faith and witness of Ulster Protestants at their best, so many of whom I have been privileged to have as friends during the many years I lived in North Antrim, my birth-place, and in Belfast. Ulster Protestants are "no petty people". It is deplorable that the obscurantist attitudes of a tiny minority, and the crimes of a small and untypical few, should ever be held to be characteristic of the vast majority of Protestants in Northern Ireland. It is no weak Christian faith which has enabled you and your fellow-Protestants to come through the attacks, physical and verbal, of which your community has been a target over the past tragic decade. It is no mean or ignoble human quality which has given you the resilience with which you have continued through these

hideous events to be, in your vast majority, good-neighbourly, good-humoured, serene and forgiving.

As a Catholic, I have felt enriched by my contacts with your tradition. I have often been inspired by your prayer, your witness, your evangelising zeal, your social and charitable concern. I have seen the fruits of Protestant faith and worship in the tradition of honest work, proud craftsmanship, respect for truth and integrity, honest dealing and sense of public service, which at their best mark the Protestant farmer and the Protestant worker, the Protestant business and professional man. Ireland would be impoverished without the truths and values enshrined in the Protestant tradition.

No coercion of Protestants

No one who knows Ulster Protestants could for a moment suppose that they can be coerced into a United Ireland, or into any other political structure, against their will. Nobody should underestimate the determination and the courage of the Northern Ireland Protestant. I shared and I share the sentiment of the late Cardinal Conway when he asked: "Who in their sober senses would want to bomb a million Protestants into a United Ireland?"

It is not simply that it would be impossible to do so. It is much more important that it would be immoral to attempt to do so. As a Catholic, and as an Irishman, I would reject with all my being and would repudiate with any power I had, any "solution" of the Irish question which would be secured through coercion by physical force or violence of the Northern Protestant community, if such were conceivable. I should no longer feel at home in an Ireland which had been "reunited" by a campaign of violence, or which would be dominated by the leaders of such a campaign or their ideas; for that Ireland would have ceased to be the country which we love and by whose noble Christian tradition and spirituality we have been formed. I wish also to assure you most earnestly that Catholics in their enormous majority deplore and detest the horrible deeds of violence, which are being perpetrated by a small number, who should be of our faith, but whose deeds bring disgrace to the name of Catholic, as well as dishonour to the name of Irishmen.

No coercion of Catholics

I beg you, in turn, as a Protestant, to accept that it would be equally immoral, and equally impossible, to coerce Northern Catholics into returning to what for them was a permanent state of "second-class citizenship". Please believe that Northern Catholics will never again consent to return to the status of a permanent political minority, excluded, as a minority, from all share in the making of the decisions on which their future social, economic and cultural welfare depend.

As a Protestant, you may yourself have experienced, under direct rule, the frustration of seeing the decisions which govern your own present and future well-being taken out of your hands and controlled by distant people, who may have little understanding of your traditions and ways, and little commitment to your cherished values. This experience bears close analogy to the experience of your Catholic fellow-Northerners through half-a-century. Surely it is possible for Protestant spokesmen to declare openly that they repudiate any solution to Northern Ireland's problems which would be secured through coercion of the Catholic community into subordinate status. Surely some Protestant spokesmen can proclaim publicly that they stand for a Northern Ireland which is shared by Protestants and Catholics in partnership and equality of civic rights and of civic responsibilities.

From coercion to reconciliation

While utterly rejecting the very idea of a solution imposed by force or coercion of one community by the other, I continue to believe that reconciliation between the two communities in the whole of Ireland, is necessary for the welfare of the island as a whole, necessary for the welfare of Catholics in Ireland, and, I submit, equally necessary for the welfare of Protestants in Ireland as a whole, and for the welfare of Northern Protestants in particular; and necessary, finally, for the welfare and peace of these islands.

In the context of today's Europe and today's Western World, the Protestant and the Catholic communities in Ireland each stand out as uniquely marked by their Christian faith and practice, and their respect for the place of religion in personal and in public life. From this point of view, Irish Catholics and Irish Protestants stand in contrast to almost any other group in Western Europe. In particular, they stand in contrast to almost any other group in our own home islands. It is incomprehensible to outside observers that we fail to realise how much we have in common, how much we resemble one another in our rejection of much of the thinking now standard in a largely secularised West. How natural and how beneficial it would be for both of us to stand together in defence of the religious values and standards which we both cherish, but which are being increasingly abandoned elsewhere, and notably in Britain.

Mutual support

As a fellow-Northerner, I would earnestly ask you to believe that no community in Western Europe or in the British Isles is likely to be as sympathetic and supportive towards your Protestant religious beliefs and principles as are Irish Catholics. Irish Protestants and Irish Catholics are religious peoples, in an increasingly non-religious Western World. They hope to remain so; but they need each other's help to remain so. Very few outside Ireland today, and especially almost no one in places of political power in Europe or in Britain today, can or will want to help Irish Catholics or Irish Protestants to remain Christian. But Irish Catholics and Irish Protestants can and must help one another to stay faithful to Christ in a world where more and more people walk away from him.

In that world, it is imbecile to suppose that Protestantism would gain through Catholicism's loss, or vice versa. Protestants will not benefit through a decline in Catholic faith; Catholics will not gain through a weakening of Protestant faith: only post-Christian secularism and materialism will flourish if either of our faith-communities declines. For each of us, what weakens the other also maims ourselves.

The visit of Pope John Paul II

The Catholic people of Ireland, North and South, are preparing for the coming visit of Pope John Paul II. They are trying to prepare in a spirit of prayer, repentance and Christian renewal. They are making prayer for peace and reconciliation one of the great preoccupations of these weeks of waiting. I feel confident that many Protestants will associate themselves spiritually with us in this effort of prayer and of repentance.

As we Catholic Bishops have said, in our Pastoral Letter to our people in preparation for this papal visit, Pope John Paul is coming to Ireland as a messenger of peace and reconciliation. His unqualified commitment to peace and to ecumenical reconciliation is well known. His rejection of violence and of terrorism is resolute and unequivocal. He has said:

> Violence generates violence; hatred generates hatred; and both of them humiliate and degrade the human person.

We Bishops have said to our people:

> May Pope John Paul's visit speak to the hearts and consciences of all those engaged in campaigns of violence and bring them back to awareness of the horrible evil of murder and to the sense of the absolute sacredness of human life. May these coming weeks of spiritual preparation for Pope John Paul's visit to Ireland not be marred by any more deeds of killing, of armed robbery or of violence. Such deeds are abominable at any time. In these weeks, they have a special element of outrage and of scandal. They are an affront to the occasion for which we are preparing. They show contempt for the feelings of the people of Ireland.

With great sadness, and indeed with anguish, we confess that, as recent events have shown, there is little hope, humanly speaking, that men inured to the ways of murder and destruction will be moved by our pleas now, any more than they have been moved by our repeated implorations in the past. Perhaps they will listen to Pope John Paul.

In one of the truly historic speeches of our time, the speech he made at Auschwitz or Oswiecim, on 7 June last, Pope John Paul quoted the words of his predecessor, Pope Paul VI:

> No more war, war never again. It is peace, peace which must guide the destinies of peoples and of all mankind.

Pope John Paul went on:

> Never one at the other's expense, at the cost of the enslavement of the other, at the cost of conquest, outrage, exploitation and death . . .

Holy is God! Holy and strong! Holy Immortal One! From plague, from famine, from fire and from *war* . . ., deliver us, Lord. Amen.

Such will be the Pope's prayer in Ireland too. The most fervent hope and prayer of the Catholic Bishops of Ireland is that his prayer for us may be heard, his plea to our men of violence may be listened to, his visit may be a new beginning of peace and partnership in our island. In the name of Christ, he will ask it. May it be so, by the power of Christ, "whose power, working in us, can do infinitely more than we can ask or imagine" (*Ephesians* 3:20).

Facing the future in hope

Christian faith is inseparably linked with Christian hope. It is not permissible for a Christian to abandon hope. Our past, and especially our recent past, gives many grounds for discouragement. But it also has lessons full of promise. One lesson from Irish history is that, when the political, social and economic and cultural deprivations and discriminations which cause inter-community strife are removed, the strife itself passes away. Another consoling lesson is that, when relations between Britain and Ireland are established on a basis of equal dignity and equal respect, a spontaneous friendship between our two peoples asserts itself. The same will apply again in the future, in the relations between the two historic communities in Ireland itself, and the relations between Ireland and Britain. The future is one of hope. The Protestant theologian, Oscar Cullmann, said:

> Christian faith is faith in the victory of Jesus Christ. It implies that the crisis of faith through which we are passing now must have a meaning in God's plan of salvation. It is for us to discharge together our obligations as Christians in the places and the times where God has willed us to be. This is our ecumenical task.

This is your task and mine as Irish Christians, divided by many differences, yet united in that which we both regard as the deepest value in our lives, our allegiance to Christ, the Lord. That Lord reigns. He is the Lord of all our Churches; and all our futures meet in him.

SOURCES AND REFERENCES

CHAPTER 1

Quotations in this chapter are taken from:

Violence in Ireland: A Report to the Churches, revised edition, C.J.L., Belfast, and Veritas, Dublin, 1977

"The Colony", John Hewitt, in *Community Forum,* Vol. 2, 1973

Constitution on the Church in the Modern World, Vatican II, Chapman, London, 1966

Integrated Schooling

Northern Ireland: Constitutional Proposals, H.M.S.O., 1973

"The Sources of Conflict", Dr James Russell, in *The Northern Teacher,* 1974

"Northern Ireland: Socialisation into Conflict", Dr James Russell, in *Social Studies,* Vol. 4, Summer 1975

Human Society in Ethics and Politics, Bertrand Russell, George Allen and Unwin Ltd, London, 1954

Mixed Marriages

Matrimonia Mixta, Motu Proprio, Pope Paul VI, Vatican Press, Rome, 1970

Pastoral Letter of the Church of Ireland Bishops on Mixed Marriages, 1966

Religion and Demographic Behaviour in Ireland, Brendan M. Walsh, Economic and Social Research Institute, Dublin, 1970

"Trends in the Religious composition of the Population in the Republic of Ireland, 1946-1971", Brendan M. Walsh, in *The Economic and Social Review,* July 1975

CHAPTER 2

Quotations in this chapter are taken from:

Collected Poems, Patrick Kavanagh, Martin, Brien and O'Keeffe, London, 1972

Message for World Peace Day 1975, Pope Paul VI

The Future of Northern Ireland — A paper for Discussion, (the "Green Paper"), H.M.S.O., 1972

Belfast: Areas of Special Social Need, Report by Project Team, H.M.S.O., 1976

CHAPTER 3

Quotations in this chapter are taken from:

Violence in Ireland and Christian Conscience, Cahal B. Daly, Veritas, Dublin, 1973

Message for World Day of Peace 1974, Pope Paul VI

One Word of Truth . . . (The Nobel Speech), Alexander Solzhenitsyn, The Bodley Head, London, 1972

Collected Poems of W. B. Yeats, W. B. Yeats, Macmillan, London, 1950

CHAPTER 4

Quotations in this chapter are taken from:

Ancient Christian Writers: the works of St Patrick, St Secundinus, Ludwig Bieler (trans.), Longman, Green and Co., London, 1953

Further Reading on "Integrated Schooling"

Education and Enmity — the control of schooling in Northern Ireland 1920-1950, Donald Harman Akenson, David and Charles (Holdings) Ltd, 1973

Catholic Schools, a survey of a Northern Ireland problem, J. J. Campbell, Fallons, Belfast, 1964

Catholic Schools, William Cardinal Conway, Veritas, Dublin, 1970

Conflict in Northern Ireland, the development of a polarised Community, John Darby, Gill and Macmillan, Dublin, 1976

"Is the Irish Conflict Religious?", John Fulton, in *Social Studies,* Vol. 5, Winter 1976-1977

Teachers and Religious Education, J. E. Greer, Religious Education Council, 1973

Address to Trinity College Theological Society, Most Rev. H. R. McAdoo, 24 October 1977

Governing without concensus — an Irish Perspective, Richard Rose, Faber and Faber, London, 1971

Attitudes in Protestant and Roman Catholic School Children in Belfast, John Salters

Segregation in Ireland – a conference organised by N.U.U., May 1978, (Contributors include:- John Darby, Alan Robinson, John Greer, Sean O'Connor, Eric Gallagher, Michael Dallat, Cahal Daly, Hugh Sockett).

Sermons on Subjects of the Day, John H. Cardinal Newman, Rivingtons, London, 1885

CHAPTER 5

Quotations in this chapter are taken from:

Human Life is Sacred, Pastoral Letter of the Irish Catholic Bishops, 1977

CHAPTER 6

Quotations in this chapter are taken from:

Redemptor Hominis, Pope John Paul II, Vatican Press, 1979

Obedience to Authority, Stanley Milgram, Tavistock Press, London, 1974

CHAPTER 7

Quotations in this chapter are taken from:

Violence in Ireland: A Report to the Churches, revised edition, C.J.L., Belfast, and Veritas, Dublin, 1977

Populorum Progressio, Pope Paul VI, C.T.S., Dublin, 1967

CHAPTER 8

Quotations in this chapter are taken from:

The Future of Northern Ireland – A Paper for Discussion (the "Green Paper"), H.M.S.O., 1972

CHAPTER 9

Quotations in this chapter are taken from:

Message for World Day of Peace 1968, Pope Paul VI, Vatican Press, 1968

Message for World Day of Peace 1979, Pope John Paul II, Vatican Press, 1979

Facing Death, Alfred Delp, Bloomsbury, 1962

CHAPTER 10

Quotations in this chapter are taken from:

The Policies of Legitimacy, Frank Burton, Routledge, London, 1978

"The Sources of Conflict", Dr James Russell in *The Northern Teacher,* 1974

"Northern Ireland: Socialisation in Conflict", Dr James Russell, in *Social Studies,* Vol. 4, Summer 1975

"Studies in Nineteenth Century Sectarian Conflict", John White, (unpublished)

Violence in Ireland: A Report to the Churches, revised edition, C.J.L., Belfast, and Veritas, Dublin, 1977

Northern Ireland: Constitutional Proposals, H.M.S.O., 1973

CHAPTER 11

Quotations in this chapter are taken from:

Ireland awaits Pope John Paul, Pastoral Letter of the Irish Catholic Bishops, Veritas, Dublin, 1979

PROVENANCE AND DATES OF TEXTS

In each case, in addition to new material, the listed Addresses are also drawn upon.

CHAPTER 1

1. Address to the Dublin University Historical Society in 1975 with the title "The Role and Responsibility of the Churches in the Northern Crisis".

2. Address delivered at Magee College, Derry, under the auspices of the Institute of Further Education of the New University of Ulster, with the title "Sepatate Schools: Distinctiveness without Divisiveness".

3. Address on Mixed Marriages, delivered at the first Ballymascanlon Inter-Church Meeting, 1973, with the title "Inter-Church Marriages: The Position of the Irish Episcopal Conference".

CHAPTER 2

1. Address to the Ecumenical "Brudermahl" of the Evangelical Church of the Rhineland and the Catholic Diocese of Essen, in April 1973.

2. Address to the Longford Association in London, August 1974.

3. Address to the Speaker's Club, Clonmel, with the title "The Christian in Politics".

CHAPTER 3

Address (the first Newman Lecture) to the Newman Society in Aquinas Hall, Belfast, with the title "Reason and Emotion in our Use of Words".

CHAPTER 4

1. Address with the same title delivered in Longford, at a celebration on 18 March 1974, in preparation for the 1975 Holy Year.

2. Address at the St Patrick's Night Dinner of the City of Sparks, Nevada, Bicentennial Committee, 17 March 1976.

CHAPTER 5

    1.   Article with this title in the *Catholic Herald,* April 1974.

    2.   Address with the same title, following a Peace Walk in Navan, December 1974.

    3.   Homily, with the title "Justice through Peace", in St Anthony's Friary Church, Athlone, for the seven hundred and fiftieth Anniversary of the Death of St Francis of Assisi, 4 October 1976.

    4.   Interview with James Downey, published in the *Irish Times,* 16 August 1976.

CHAPTER 6

    1.   Address in Longford, for World Peace Day 1977, with the title "Peace and the Sacredness of Human Life".

    2.   Address to the Social Study Conference in Kilkenny in August 1974, with the title "Conformity and Conscience".

CHAPTER 7

Address in Longford on World Peace Day 1978, with the title "The Politics of Peace".

CHAPTER 8

    1.   Article in the *Catholic Herald,* 14 January 1977, with the title "Northern Ireland: the British Dimension".

    2.   Address to members of Pax Christi in London in April 1978, with the title "Northern Ireland: a Shared Responsibility".

CHAPTER 9

Address with the same title in Longford on World Peace Day 1979.

CHAPTER 10

Address with the same title to the English Commission on International Justice and Peace, London, 1 September 1979.

CHAPTER 11

An unpublished text.

SCRIPTURE REFERENCES

INDEX